ETERNAL LIVING NOW

SCRIPTURAL ETERNALITY

BY

ROLAND RUFFIN

www.EternalLivingNow.com
Eternallivingnow77@gmail

Special Thanks to Pennie, my wife and Leshanea and Lanique, my daughters, for their support, patience, and love, during the construction of this book.

I am deeply grateful for the editing advice, insights, and prayer support, received from my Eternal Living Now Bible Study and Focus Group.

May God, bless you all for your labor of love...

The Author

Roland Ruffin is a graduate of Bishop College and the American Baptist Seminary of the West with a MDIV and B.A. in Theology and Pastoral Care. Reverend Ruffin served as a fulltime State Chaplain for 30 years with the California Department of Corrections and Rehabilitation.

This book, entitled, *Scriptural Eternality,* was written to help Believers in Christ, to develop disciplined study approaches, to identifying, researching, and applying, the eternal truths and revelations of God to His people. Every page of this book, focuses on providing information, relative to the eternality of God, in heaven, or earth. God's desire for His people to know Him intimately, requires insightful knowledge and experience of God's eternal Nature, Throne room communication, and Divine identity, that is eternally in-Christ, within you and me. The objectives of this book, are to stimulate, and motivate, the people of God, into studying the scriptures, for exploration of eternal realities that surround us. Our goal is to create a comfort level of scripture study, through an Eternal Lens, so that we can perceive, believe, and behave, the eternality of God's endless blessings, both in this world, and the new heaven and earth to come.

FOREWORD

"Scriptural Eternality," was written as a continuation of the Eternal Living Now study series. My first book, entitled, *"The Introduction to Eternal Living Now,"* followed by the next book, entitled, *"Eternal Living Now (Intermediate Level),"* followed by this book, *"Eternal Living Now (Scriptural Eternality),"* all contribute to the ever-evolving development of resources, for comprehensive studies on the eternality of God in the bible and within His people.

Eternal Living Now, is a vision that God gave to me and my wife, that informs and reveals the eternality of God's salvation, our lives in-Christ, and the eternal meaning, message, ministry of Christ in heaven, on earth.

The goal of Scriptural Eternality is to inform, inspire, and motivate cursory readers of the bible to become scriptural investigators, who search for the eternal truths, and messages that God predestined for our discovery in His Word.

God revealed His eternal heart, through His eternal Spirit, to His eternal people, for an everlasting relationship, both in and beyond this present world. Spiritual Eternality will help us to develop a discipline of discovering the eternal gems of the eternality of Divine activity in heaven, on earth, in-Christ, within you and me.

Reading the bible through an *Eternal Lens*, has become a life-changing discipline for everyone in the Focus Group for the development of this book. We hope, this will be your testimony as well upon the conclusion of reading and completing the exercises in this book.

TABLE OF CONTENTS

CHAPTER ONE

ETERNALITY IN OUR SCRIPTURES

Our God is an eternal God, Who desires an everlasting relationship with His household in heaven or earth. Eternality is the key to understanding what a healthy relationship looks like through the *lens* of the Divine. Mankind was never created to just exist for a second, then die and never exist again. Things that were not created in the Image and Likeness of God, may be relegated to that of perishable value. But Adam (mankind), was created in the non-perishable eternal Image, and Likeness, of Yahweh-Elohim, the eternal Self-existing Persona-Creator God. The incubation, of the Divine exhaled breath of intelligence and animated life within Adam's body of clay, was never meant to mirror his Creator at the perishable level of an animal, rock, or breeze of air. Mankind, was created in the Image and Likeness of our *eternal* God for an *eternal* relationship, from heaven through earth, to an eternal heavenly earth. This is the reason why eternality, regarding relationship with God, and the Kingdom of God, saturates the scriptures as its foundation for interaction with God. Eternality, is not always noticeable, visible, or apparent, but almost always present and replete, within the fabric of scriptural events in our Bible. Remember, our eternal God, ultimately deals with humanity from an eternal perspective, regardless the generation or century. In fact, we cannot even perceive ourselves as the image and likeness of our eternal God, without factoring eternality into the equation. Our eternal God, Who ultimately originates humanity for an everlasting relationship with Himself, is the entirety of the biblical message from Genesis through Revelation.

Since eternality, relative to Divine Persona, salvation in-Christ, and the everlasting blessings, revelations, relationships, and heavenly realities on earth, is the primary focus of this book, then a working definition of the *"eternal"* is warranted before we go any further. A working definition of the *"eternal"* includes, *what exist before the creation of time, exist within time, and what exist through and beyond the limits of time."* Yes, there are other academic definitions of the "eternal," but the simple, comprehensive, and inclusive definition, just provided, adequately covers the basis required for this book. Since our focus will major on the process of locating eternality within the fabric of our scriptures, then a definition for the word *exegesis* (pulling out of scripture), *eisegesis* (reading into scriptures), and *hermeneutics* (art/science of scripture interpretation), in addition to our *limited use* of the processes represented by each of these words, is also warranted. By definition, exegesis involves the attempt to explain what the text meant in the original literary and socio-historical setting for its original writer and audience. A simple working definition is that exegesis, is the attempt to interpret scriptures, as close to the context of its original language and meaning, as possible. Since we cannot go back to B.C. or A.D., it is impossible to interpret ancient scriptures in our bible with 100% accuracy. Because of our human nature, our words, phrases, and original intentions in our writings and documentations, are in a constant state of interpretive evolution. Even in our present century, certain words, may have the same spelling, but with different pronunciations or meanings based upon our geographical location and dialect of language. Example, the word attaché' suitcase. It can be pronounced three different ways depending on what region of America you live in, let alone the rest of the world. A century from now, historians will probably record only one pronunciation for the word "attaché." Future generations will only know the single pronunciation of "attaché, that is provided by the linguist of their language, even though this word is pronounced three different ways in our present generation. It will be impossible for future generations, to know the exact meanings of the vocabulary of our present milieu because of the constant changing, and evolving, nature of human language. There is no way to know, with total precision, the exact meaning of any words that were used over one or two thousand years ago in our bible. However, we can know the approximate meanings, and intentions of ancient words and phrases, through scholarly research and revelation from the Holy Spirit. The *limited* exegetical process presented in this book, is expected to produce approximate word-for-word, and thought-for-thought understandings of what was penned from the author's personal perspective, in addition to the information the author wanted his audience to receive from his writings.

Although passages of scriptures will be reviewed in this book from a *limited* exegetical perspective, this author informs the reader up front, that this book will begin and end with perspectives that are based upon interpretation of scripture through an *Eternal Lens* for intentional *awareness,* of *eternal outcomes.* This means that time will not be expended in this book, to present a false pretense of neutrality towards scripture as the disposition of this author. I repeat, scientific neutrality towards the scripture, is not the goal of this author. My intention, is to view scripture through a *Lens of Eternality,* which means a limited practice of eisegesis, will be included in the interpretation of scriptures by default. Also, some principles of hermeneutics, relative to *identification* and *participation* with eternal realities from eisegesis perspectives, will be presented in Chapters

Three and Four. It is my deliberate intention to motivate, inspire, and incentivize, readers to begin reading the bible through an *Eternal Lens,* as we seek to understand the relevance of the eternality of our God in our daily experiences of life. It is time to balance our cultural approach to the scriptures, which often majors on the value of the ephemeral and temporary, with the everlasting values of eternality in our bible. For example, you probably already know how to pray to God for a bigger paycheck, deliverance from enemies, or other ephemeral needs. As we are grateful for the privilege of prayer, we are also encouraged to know that eternal realities in-Christ, are far greater than learning how to pray to pay an electric bill, or for purchasing top brand clothing as a Divine inheritance. The endless resources, that are available in-Christ, far exceed the ephemeral and temporary appetites of our present cultural conditioning. Awakening appetites for fulfillment, through everlasting experiences in-Christ, is our earnest desire for everyone who reads this book. Eternality, and eternal values, is, and shall intentionally remain, our primary focus throughout this book, without apology.

The word, "*eternality*," is extremely important from a biblical perspective, because our eternal God has provided eternal blessings, resources, functions, and guidance, that culminate in the ultimate maturity and evolution of humanity, as a new species of existence, in-Christ. Jesus rose from the dead as a new eternal species, a new first fruits from the dead, and a new creation that can never die because this new species transcended death forever through resurrection power. I am sure you know that the new species, that Christ is and will be forever, is the new species that you have become through your born-again transformation, in-Christ. As you became a new creation in-Christ, through belief and confession of faith in Jesus as your savior (Rom 10:9), the spiritual experience of the Holy Spirit, that converted your human spirit, into His eternal Nature (1Cor 6:17), transformed your spirit-soul-body connection, into a receptacle for the authentic, eternal Nature of Christ, to indwell (See my book on the *Introduction to Eternal Living Now* for more information on spiritual-soul). The authentic Nature of

Christ will indwell within your spirit-soul, as well as your raptured or resurrected material body forever, because the Nature of Christ is forever, eternal.

So, as you begin looking at the bible through the *Lens of Eternality*, every book, chapter, parable, episode, and event in the bible becomes an opportunity to see the possibility of eternal messages and revelations behind the scenes. Remember, God is eternal. He communicates eternally through His Spirit; therefore, we want to learn how to discern, research, perceive the eternality of God's thoughts, ways, revelations, and inspirations to His people, from heaven to earth through the scriptures.

Most of the scriptures in our bible, that express Divine thoughts, or begin with *"Thus saith the Lord,"* originate from the mind of the eternal Spirit of God (2 Tim 3:16). In other words, our bible is replete with thoughts that were revealed from the heart of our eternal God to mankind through His eternal Spirit, for directives in eternal living, on earth, or in heaven. Commit the word, "eternality" to memory, as this word will be echoed throughout this entire book with the expectation, that familiarity and association with this word, will eventually become personal assimilation and companionship with eternality before you complete this book. Eternality, flows with God because it is *of* and *from*, our eternal God. The opportunity to flow in agreement with the course and activity of eternality in our world, is a priceless opportunity to adopt, assimilate, and personify, the Nature of Divine eternality that governs, fulfills, and direct our lives, in-Christ.

Give yourself permission to develop an appetite for researching, pursuing, discerning, and perceiving, eternal realities of God's thoughts, blessings, revelations, and everlasting truths as a reference point for your review of each chapter in our bible. The lens you see through, affects the reality of what you see. Please permit yourself to see through the *Lens of Eternality*, so that we will begin to see, communicate, and associate, with our God, eternally, and not just ephemerally.

CHAPTER TWO

PERSONAL RELEVANCE OF ETERNALITY

What makes us the eternal people of God, is the residence of the Divine Nature of God within us by His Spirit. This fact is extremely important if you plan on living in God's heavenly household forever, because only the Nature of God dominates His household in heaven, or earth, eternally. God will never have a foreign or competing nature in His household, ever again, as Lucifer/Satan and adherents of his rebellious nature, were cast out of heaven (Luke 10:18). To exist, or remain, as a resident of the household of God in heaven or earth, one must exist *in*, and *as* the Nature of God.

ETERNALITY DESIRES THE ETERNAL

The ultimate *desires* of the eternal Nature of the Divine, are "eternal." Jesus revealed the *Law of Sameness*, when he said, "*that, which is born of flesh, is flesh*, and *that which is born of spirit, is spirit*" (Jn 3:6). In other words, *sameness*, is an indicator of uniformity, as well as the *desires* unique to this uniformity. The eternal Nature of God *desires*, what is uniformly *within* the eternal Nature of Himself. Likewise, eternality is also the deepest desire of the human soul that desires existence in uniformity with the Image and Likeness, of the Divine. This is the reason why Solomon said that mankind was "*created to desire eternity*" (Eccl 3:11). The ephemeral and temporary experiences of life, will never provide ultimate satisfaction of fulfillment, because the desires of our spiritual souls, are eternal. Newsflash! Bible study, that majors on the discovery of temporary solutions and revelations, will not provide ultimate personal fulfillment for our eternal desires. Our God focused on our deepest needs as He provided eternal solutions, blessings, and meaningful revelations within the fabric of our scriptures, that await our prospecting efforts to locate the gold of their eternal value and worth. Only eternality within the scriptures, can satisfy the desires of the everlasting Nature we have in-Christ. We simply must look deeper, dig deeper, and prospect deeper, in order to get to the ultimate gold of the scriptures, that are always based upon eternality.

HEAVENLY FUTURE IN OUR PRESENT NOW

Our God provided eternal truths, from heaven to earth, so that we could participate as companions with His eternal agenda regarding the transformation of our planet, into an everlasting heavenly earth (Rev 11:15). Might I remind you, that the heavenly earth (the future society of heaven and earth, as one society), will be an eternal, everlasting society according to Revelation 22. Our destination, culminates into an eternal, everlasting destiny. This is why we are learning how to live, think, walk, talk, exist eternally now, because we are members of an eternal community and society in-Christ, both now, and forever. Why would God prepare us for the future, with only a temporary relationship with Himself in our present now? Why would He allow us to only experience temporary realities of an eternal relationship, if eternity is both our destination and destiny? Existing as a Christian only to survive, though popular today, is really not eternal living! Eternality is the existence of eternal life. Eternality is the experience of the infinite, the impossible, and the timeless, rather than experiencing only the limits of time and perishable possessions as popularized in our culture. Eternal living, in-Christ, is living realities, that are everlasting in our present now. However, we cannot live the realities of eternality if we do not know them. We can live like paupers, though we may be millionaires, if we are unaware of wealth in our bank account. We must be willing to dig deeper, dig beyond the surface of scriptural episodes, and discover the rich deposits of the gold of eternality, that is often concealed within the fabric of the scriptures. *"Seek and ye shall"* find eternality in our scriptures, and the rewards of your discoveries will result in personal fulfillment that far exceeds the temporary self-gratifications, offered in our culture.

As we learn how to discover eternal truths and realities that are located within the fabric of our scriptures, we will be challenged to choose to align ourselves with the purposes and activities of eternal realities in heaven, that also operate on our earth. The eternality of the everlasting, originates from our eternal God, for a purpose. God has established eternal operations, and activities in our world, in order to bring about the fulfillment of His promises regarding His ultimate everlasting, and endless, new world order of a heavenly earth. God intends for His present heavenly society, to transform earth into an endless heavenly society, so that both Divine households in heaven and earth, can become one eternal household, residing in one new heaven and earth location (Matt 6:10). Our eternal God, is controlling, shifting, bending events on earth, towards fulfillment of His ultimate eternal Will. Divine, eternal activity, is acting upon life in our universe, daily. We have opportunities to participate, and partner, with the eternal activities of God for shared eternal outcomes, every single day. Personal participation in the eternal love of God, eternal peace of God, joy of God, healing of God, compassion of God, goodness of God, etc., results in your personal edification and maturity as a bonus. For example, participation _with_ the joy of the Lord, includes personal edification, _in_ the joy of Lord. More than the experience of eternal blessings, i.e., Divine joy, or peace, we also experience the *satisfaction*, and *fulfillment*, that only the eternality of God can provide because of the fulfilling presence of eternality, in-Christ, through His Spirit within each born-again citizen of His Kingdom.

PERSONAL EDIFICATION OF ETERNALITY

The love of God is eternal because God is eternal. The peace of God is everlasting because God is everlasting. Jesus revealed the eternal love, and everlasting peace of God on earth, to afford opportunities for the eternality of Divine love and peace to operate in our world thru us, and ultimately AS us. As partnership with the Divine *evolves* to everlasting love and peace *within* us, *through* us, and finally *AS* us, our sensitivity to eternality, increases in conscious awareness. The more awareness we have of the tremendous magnitude of each blessing in eternality, the more we can appreciate what we already have in-Christ. The magnitude of transformation that occurs in-Christ for each of us, can only be measured eternally. As we partner with the transformative activity of eternality, transformation also occurs within, and around us. This means that the benefits we receive from participation with eternality, also benefit our world by default. We are enlarged with Divine peace, as we partner with the activity of Divine peace in our world. The world becomes better, because through partnership with eternal activities, we become better.

Christ did not come to our earth to minister earthly solutions for earthly results. Christ came to earth, to minister eternal solutions (eternal life), for eternal outcomes (everlasting Kingdom of God).

IN-CHRIST, ETERNALITY IS THE SOLUTION, BEYOND TEMPORARY ADVERSITIES.

Remember the temporary, is simply moments of eternity, or ephemeral time, in eternal timelessness. Fixation with adversities in time, is not our goal. As Christ majored on revealing the eternal interest of the Father in heaven to our world, we are to do the same. Revealing the eternal interest of God in this world, does not have to be laborious. In fact, sharing the eternal thoughts and desires of our Father in heaven on earth, can be exciting, desirable, and as fulfilling as a delicious meal. Jesus said, *"my meat (food) is to do the will of Him who sent me, and to finish His work"* (Jn 4:34). Tasty meals are very satisfying, especially when we are really hungry. Imagine the degree of satisfaction that we could experience, as awareness of the value of the Will of God is increased to the degree, where surrender and accomplishment of His Will, equates to endless personal satisfaction and fulfillment. Developing a disciplined desire and appetite for investigating, appreciating, and accommodating, the activities of eternality, is rewarded with a spiritual joy, that exceeds the satisfaction, received from our best cuisine. *"O taste and see that the Lord is good,"* is a very true statement, because the more we understand the eternal realities of God, the better we enjoy our existence in-Christ, within our world. Deeper understanding of the eternality of God, leads to greater appreciation for the deliciousness of Divine knowledge, and the sweetness of eternal wisdom that makes you dig deeper for more.

In-Christ, time becomes opportunity to experience more of the eternal, even if experiencing the eternal through the ephemeral is required. Within the realms of eternality, one can discover, Divine solutions beyond ephemeral adversities, that are worth being fixated upon. Researching the scriptures for eternal truths, can be a joyous experience. Receiving revelations from the Spirit of God during study times, can inspire the desire for more understanding of the eternal, through and beyond the ephemeral. Time is never lost, during the study of eternality in our bible, because eternality, is what sustains the existence of time. We have all to gain, and nothing to lose for the time we expend in participation, partnership, and companionship with the eternal activities of God in our world. Allow the joy of the Lord to saturate your soul during each time of scriptural study.

ENVISIONING ETERNALITY IN YOUR LIFE

A wise time planner, told us to *"start our beginning, with the end in mind."* In other words, know how you want to end, before you begin. Have a vision of what the end-goal, and final achievement, look like, before you begin to work your plan. The reason homes have blueprints, is because the builders must know what the conclusion of their work should look like, before the first brick is ever laid. What does fulfillment of the eternal desires of God, in-Christ, within you, look like? How do you think, the eternal joy of the Lord, should look on you? What about the eternal love, peace, righteousness, goodness, mercy, abundance, greatness, righteousness, or patience of God, as your persona, because of your participation with the Divine? Could the experience of God in heaven, be satisfying for you, on earth? Could the meaning and activity of God's approval of you in heaven, be enough for self-approval, on earth? Do you have a vision of who you can be, fully clothe with the Persona of God, walking in full agreement with the Spirit of Christ, Who brings the truth in heaven into our earth, for heavenly results in our world? As eternal activities, are already changing, and transforming our world into the Kingdom of God, have you already imagined what you look like, as a transparent vehicle of eternality in heaven, on earth? Please take time, if you have not already, to visualize a clear picture of what culmination, satisfaction and fulfillment, in-Christ, could possibly look like in your life, as you continue reading this book. A view, vision, idea or at least a dream, of what the final outcome of your participation with eternal activities could look like in your life, should be a major pursuit and achievement, as you exegete scriptures through an *Eternal Lens*.

CHAPTER THREE

THE PRACTICE OF LOCATING ETERNALITY IN THE BIBLE

Some people made fortuncs in America during the Gold mining age of the 1800s. If you were going to be successful in gold mining, it was profitable to be familiar with certain words that were well known by the rich. One important word to know, was the word called *"prospect."* The *Prospecting Process*, included researching and locating areas that held the most promise for deposits of gold. This required logic, planning, vision, expectation, and implementation of action plans in order to maximize success, while avoiding wasted time and resources. Opportunities for prospecting was afforded to Adam as God placed gold, under the ground in the Garden of Eden for eventual discovery through digging, searching, and industrious exercises (Gen 2:12). Yes, Adam would have to dig beyond the surface of the dirt, in order to get to the hidden golden goodies in the Garden, but wouldn't the imperishable nature and value of gold, be worth the effort? Likewise, the discovery of eternality, within the fabric of our scriptures, is at least equal to, if not more valuable, than all of the gold in the Garden of Eden.

The *Prospecting Process* for this book, begins with agreement with an initial unction, received from the eternal Spirit of God (1 Jn 2:20). Why? Because the inclusion of eternality within the fabric of our scriptures, originated from and through the eternal Spirit of God (2 Tim 3:16). As the Spirit of God in heaven revealed the thoughts of God from heaven to earth, we must remember that God's thought(s) do not originate through the human mind, but the Mind of our eternal God. For example, eternal thoughts, revelations, meanings, and purposes were communicated by God's eternal Spirit to prophets, sages, writers, preachers, teachers, seers, kings, priest, men, women, boys and girls, throughout the scriptures in order to reveal the eternality of Divine intentions to mankind. The eternal Spirit of God, Who originated the scriptures, is really the only Person qualified to guide us into the eternal treasures that are concealed within the bible. *It takes the eternal to reveal the eternal.* I reiterate, the original author of our scriptures, Who is the eternal Spirit of God, knows were the gold of eternality is located within the scriptures. The human mind is incapable of determining every location of eternality in our scriptures. The eternal Spirit of God came to earth to guide us into all truth. That truth includes the location, identification, and application of eternality within the Word of God for Divine glorification, personal edification, and global transformation.

Unction from the Holy Spirit, most often occurs intuitively and internally, rather than mechanically or externally. Our bible, originated from Eastern culture, not Western. The Eastern concept of God, speaking within us, is more real than external conversation around us. Communication from the Spirit of God within us, is a felt-awareness, a moving-involvement, an experience of Divine presence that fills us within, an inner-voice, an intuitive vocalized passion, the silence of sound that can be heard within the heart, it is reality within us, that is greater than reality outside of us. These examples may be difficult to grasp by Western minds. However, they are experienced each day subconsciously. You have probably heard that over 80% of our conscious behavior is governed or influenced by our sub-conscious mind. Much of what we see with our eyes, is governed by what is concealed and unseen within our unconscious mind. We often hear our own internal voice quietly speaking to us during the process of making decisions on a daily basis. Hearing voices internally, is nothing new. However, being led by the *experience* of the Spirit of God, is a progressive growth in *awareness of the eternality of God's Person.* Conscious awareness of the eternality of the Persona of God may be new for some of us. This book encourages you to develop intimate sensitivity in hearing the Spirit of God within your in-Christ, relationship daily. The Spirit of God will guide you to the scriptures that incubate eternality because God's desire is for you to know, align, participate, and companion, with His eternal activity in heaven on earth, through His Word. As there was gold underneath the ground upon which Adam stood in the Garden, there is also the gold of eternality beneath, and within, the scriptures of our bible, awaiting our discovery, through industrious digging.

THE GOLD OF ETERNALITY

Locating the *gold of eternality* in our scriptures is our first priority in the *Prospecting Process*. Next, upon receiving an unction from the Holy Spirit concerning a certain word, phrase, or passage of scriptural gold, we must proceed to *digging out* the *gold of eternality,* and separating the gold (eternality), from the ephemeral (temporary). In actual gold mining, the raw gold was often heated or melted in order to get rid of unnecessary elements that were attached to it under the ground. The dross, or elements that were discarded or burned off, were still valuable for other purposes, but the desire was to remove all dross so that only pure gold would remain. As we learn how to separate scriptures that reveal eternality from scriptures that only refer to timely events, we develop a list of eternal verses for our everlasting vocabulary that may be progressively used, in service of mature articulation of eternal language. Finally, through our *Prospecting Process*, determination of what is relevant to our need and the needs of others, will help us prioritize the words we need to research, as we transition from the *Prospecting Process to* **R**udiments **o**f **R**esearch exercises.

The refining process of gold exposes its purity while allowing for the discovery of original scripture, in context to its historical setting. This process is called the **R**udiments **o**f **R**esearch.

THE RUDIMENTS OF RESEARCH

The **R**udiments **o**f **R**esearch includes a personal strategy for basic research exercises, utilization of research tools, resources, possible interpretation, and application of research outcomes, that will benefit our global society.

Once we have completed the *Prospecting Process* under the unction of the Holy Spirit, then we will proceed to **R**udiments **o**f **R**esearch for further development of eternal implications hidden within the fabric of our scriptural passage.

PREPARATION FOR RUDIMENT OF RESEARCH EXERCISES

Word research, requires tools that every student of the Bible should possess. The tools recommended in this Chapter, will assist you in identifying the shared meaning of the scriptures presented by the author during their lifetime.

MULTIPLE BIBLE TRANSLATIONS:

Analyzing scripture(s), in multiple biblical translations, is necessary to gain a broader perspective of the author's original intent. I recommend comparing your translation with at least five other translations. The goal is to understand what the words in your text meant to the author, and the author's audience via literal word-for-word bible translations. The following: *New American Standard Bible (NASB), New Revised Standard Version (NRSV), Revised Standard Version (RSV), New English Translation (NET), English Standard Version (ESV), and the New King James Version (NKJV)*, are all good Greek and Hebrew word-for-word translation resources.

Looking at your text, side-by-side, with each version, will help you better determine the intention of the author's words, even though the words in each translation may be slightly different.

Paraphrased translations such as the Amplified Bible, Phillips version, The Living Bible, the Passion Translation of the Bible, etc., are recommended for less critical study of the scriptures, as they tend to focus on thought-for-thought translation of Hebrew and Greek words, thus decreasing their accuracy. Remember our *limited* exegesis exercise will excise meaning *from* the text (exegesis), rather than reading meaning *into* the text (eisegesis).

E-Sword.com offers free and very inexpensive Bible Software downloads to over ten different versions of the bible (*including the translations, recommended above*).

Logos.com, also offers great bible student software for less than $100.

Now, in addition to possession of word-for-word bibles, let's look at some additional tools you will need to conduct **R**udiment **of R**esearch exercises (*you should purchase at least one of each resource*):

CONCORDANCES:

- Strong's Exhaustive Concordance

- Ellison, J.W. Nelson's Complete Concordance of the RSV Bible, Thomas Nelson and Sons, 1957

- Morrison, C. An Analytical Concordance to the Revised Standard Version of the New Testament, Westminster, 1979

A concordance will provide information regarding the spelling and pronunciation of your word-selection in its original language. It will concordance will also provide various meanings of words within its biblical and historical context. Also, other words or scriptures, that emphasize the meaning of your select-word, may be provided for additional research. Finally, a concordance will provide the root or original word from which your word-selection evolved, and most often a numerical notation of where both the root-word can be further researched in a Hebrew or Greek Theological Dictionary.

BIBLE DICTIONARY:

- The Anchor Bible Dictionary

- The Interpreters Dictionary of the Bible and Supplementary Volume

- Unger's Bible Dictionary

Bible Dictionaries provide information on the historical development and present meaning of your select-word. Multi-cultural and global definitions of your select-word may be included.

INTERLINEARS:

- *Blueletterbible.org*, offers a free online Bible Interlinear

- *Biblehub.com*, also offers a free online Bible Interlinear

A Bible Interlinear, parallels the Hebrew or Greek words, with English, so that you can see exactly how the author penned your passage of scripture in its original language. Most Interlinear software, will indicate the grammatical tense of the words in your passage, i.e., noun, verb, preposition, past or perfect-tense, future-perfect tense, etc. The meaning of the words in your passage of scripture, can change dramatically, based upon its grammatical form, position, mood, or tense, in its original language.

COMMENTARIES:

- Interpretation: A Bible Commentary for Teaching and Preaching

- The Anchor Bible Commentary

- A Critical and Historical Commentary on the Bible

Commentaries provide a professional, and modern perspective, of what the words in your passage of scripture may mean within its historical context.

ATLAS AND BIBLE HANDBOOKS:

- Westermann, C. Handbook on the Old and New Testament

- Eissfeldt, O. The Old Testament: An Introduction. Harper and Row, 1965.

- Kummel, W.G. Introduction to the New Testament, Abingdon, 1975.

- The Harpers Atlas of the Bible

A Bible handbook, will provide great information on the ancient cultural and historical setting, that your author may have experienced, during the time your passage of scripture was penned. Understanding the ancient world and environment of the text, is vitally important to understanding the influence of the culture upon the author's selection of words and writing style.

WORDBOOKS:

- Theological Dictionary of the New Testament, 10 volumes. Eerdmans

- Theological Dictionary of the Old Testament, 6 volumes. Eerdmans

Bible wordbooks provide insightful information of the evolving meaning of biblical words in their original language, and their etymological progressions. This is a very useful tool, when trying to understand the word-selections of your author.

BIBLICAL THEOLOGIES:

- Bultmann, R. Theology of the New Testament, Westminster, 1961-67

- Kummel, W.G. The Theology of the New Testament according to major witnesses, Abingdon Press, 1973

- Von Rad, G. Old Testament Theology, Harper and Row, 1962-65.

Bible theology books, often provide a comprehensive interpretation of the book, in which your passage of scripture may be located. Theology, by definition is "God talk," and well-developed discussions, opinions, clarifications, and viewpoints, regarding the interpretation of God throughout the scriptures.

Most, if not all of the research tools recommended in this chapter, are available in the online bible software that was mentioned above (with additional purchases). I recommend online software, over physical book purchases, because they are less expensive, and provide easy word- search applications.

Once you are in possession of your research tools, then we are ready to engage the **R**udiments **o**f **R**esearch, after completing your *Prospecting Process*.

RUDIMENTS OF RESEARCH

Only the eternal Spirit of God, Who knows the eternal thoughts of the Father in heaven (1Cor 2:10,11), really knows where each nugget of eternality is located throughout the entire bible. *It takes the eternal, to accurately identify the eternal.* This means   only the eternal Spirit of God is qualified to guide, and identify the eternal truths, embedded in revelations of Divine thought to mankind as Scriptures. Who knows truth better than the Spirit of Truth, Who is also called the Spirit of God, and the Spirit of Christ as well (Jn 16:13; Rom 8:9, 14). The power, presence, manifestations, and embodiments of eternality in heaven, is *actualized* in our world through the Spirit of Truth. The Spirit of Truth knows how to accurately guide and reveal eternality during every study session. To attempt the *Prospecting Process* without guidance, unction, or consultation with the very Spirit Who originated the messages, revealed to authors, *"who wrote the scriptures under the inspiration of the Holy Spirit,"* is simply dangerous and futile. Also, to think that we can discover eternal truth, based upon our own *scientific methods* without revelation from the Spirit of Truth, is absurd, misleading, and unhealthy. Therefore, every utilization of the *Prospecting Process* to determine which words in scripture will become our golden nugget of focus, will be preceded by prayer, and surrender for Spiritual guidance. Let's move on to the **R**udiments **of R**esearch process.

The first step in the **R**udiments **o**f **R**esearch process, is conducting a *limited* exegesis exercise on words within your passage as scripture. Our *limited* exegesis will be followed by Hermeneutical research, i.e., Literary, Historical, and Interpretative Applications, that should look similar to the Outlay on the next pages.

OBERVATION

- Who is speaking and to whom is he speaking?
- Where or when will it happen?
- Why is something being said?
- How will this happen?

MARKING Key words and phrases

- A noun, descriptive word, or action that conveys the authors intentions

LISTS DEVELOPMENT

- All the attributes, characteristics of the main character, concepts, by observing how a key word is described.

WATCH for contrast or comparisons: Check for differences in expressions of time, environments,

IDENTIFY terms of conclusion: Wherefor, therefore, finally, but, God, (when you see wherefore, know what is therefore).

DEVELOP Chapter themes: Determine the divisions, key dates and main point as theme

DEVELOP Chapter themes: Determine the divisions, key dates and main point as theme

INTERPRETATION (that which goes with the text)

- Context is King (The verse itself, Surrounding verses, entire book, meta knowledge of the Bible for comparison). Is my interpretation of a passage of scripture consistent with the theme, purpose, and structure of the book in which it is found? Is there a glaring difference?
- Always seek the full council of the Word of God
- Scripture will never contradict Scripture as a norm (Solo Scriptura)
- Do not base your convictions on an obscure/ambiguous passage of Scripture
- Interpret scripture literally when it is literally presented but also Interpret scripture in the light of their literary style: Didactic, poetic, proverbial, similes, metaphors, literary styles.

APPLICATION

Apply scripture in the light of its teaching, reproof, instruction, and correction, (2 Tim 3:16). The bible I the foundation for interpretation of truth. What is God saying about a specific Truth (to apply) through accurate Observation and Interpretation.

- Application of Reproof (2 Tim 3:16) :

- Application of Doctrinal
- Application of Instruction
- Application of Righteousness
- Application of Good Works

The Outlay, provided above, presented key research objectives that will require familiarity, and hands-on navigating experience while transitioning from the *Prospective Process,* to Rudiments of Research conclusions.

Let's take a closer look at both *Prospective,* and **R**udiments **o**f **R**esearch processes. Major components of the *Prospecting Process,* include 1. Prayer for guidance during scriptural searches for eternal nuggets 2. Selecting scripture(s), per unction from the Holy Spirit Who is the ultimate author of our scriptures, 3. Development of a Prospect List of words, believed to be nuggets of eternality.

Once the development of our Prospect List has been completed, we are now ready to begin **R**udiments **of R**esearch exercises.

As we proceed in the **R**udiments **of R**esearch process, begin by reading two Chapters before, and after your passage of scripture to preview thoughts of your author, before and after what was penned in your passage. Now let's read your select passage of scripture, slowly, methodically, and critically, while observing repeated words, mood of the sentences, and rhythm of phrases (literary form). Our goal is to gain insight on the world of the text, through the text itself. Be sure to write down repetitive words in all of the scriptures you have read (Words were intentionally repeated for a reason by the author). While reading your select passage of scripture, we need to ask ourselves every possible question, regarding the *who, what, where, why* and *when,* as it relates to what may or may not be included in the text.

Now let's use our *Interlinear*, and *Concordance*, to understand what the words in your passage of scripture meant in their original language. Your Interlinear will provide the exact words your author penned in the text, and your Concordance will provide the definition, location and number of times your word was biblically, so you can compare words in your passage with their usage in other occurrences. Be sure to write down the Concordance definition of each word in your passage, as understood, in its original language. We are now ready to compare our Interlinear words with our Concordance notes, for language-accuracy and legitimacy. Remember, our goal at this stage of exegesis is to accurately pull meaning out of the text as it is written, without coloring it with our own modern interpretation. The original text, according to the Interlinear, and information, provided in the Concordance, should provide a more accurate foundation of what your author actually said in your passage of scripture. On a separate sheet of paper, copy each word of your passage from your Interlinear while placing the information from your Concordance under each word copied. This is a great start, as we need to see what the author is saying, rather than what we want the author to say. Write down more, *who, what, were,* and *when* questions in your mind regarding your passage of scripture, in addition to the author's intentions for writing it. We now have a basic *foundation* to build upon in our exegetical quest to understand what the author's own perspective of his writings were. Time to compare what you have written down to other bible translations of your passage of scripture.

Now, let's compare your passage of scripture side-by-side with five other word-for-word translations of your passage. How does each translations differ from what you have written down? What is the same between the translations? Now write down how the different translations support or differ from the *foundation* page you have developed. Based upon your foundation document, compared with the five translations of your passage, write down what you think were the author's intentions for each word in your passage of scripture. Place your foundation document, and personal assessment of each word penned by the author used in a safe place for future referencing. We have just conducted a *limited* exegetic exercise for beginners. Congratulate yourself.

THE HERMENEUTIC PROCESS
HANDBOOKS, ENCYCLOPEDIAS, COMMENTARIES

Now that we have exegeted meaning out of the text (exegesis), let's proceed to the hermeneutic process for interpretation of scripture. This process begins with the information, accumulated through our exegesis exercise. Let's read our passage of scripture again. This time let's observe it literary context by feeling the flow of the words in each sentence. Do the words have a poetic flow, or more of an instructional flow? Commanding or smooth? Read your passage out loud. Do the words sound like they were meant to flow poetically, preachy, or matter of fact? Write this information down for future references regarding the Literary Form of your passage.

Let's dig deeper into the world of the author's text by investigating the historical-social context of your passage of scripture. Information in your *handbook* and *encyclopedia*, regarding cultural activity during the time your author penned your passage, in addition to expert reviews of your passage by religious professional in your *commentaries*, are great resources for this area of research. Make sure to include, both the views you agree, and disagree with, in your personal notes. Keep these notes in a safe place for future references.

THE HERMENEUTIC PROCESS: THEOLOGY BOOKS, WORDBOOKS, BIBLE DICTIONARIES, ATLASES

Now let's look at theological positions and interpretations of your passage of scripture from religious professionals for different perspectives. Your theology books will provide scholarly viewpoints, that may be useful in your efforts to responsibly interpret your passage. Let's combine the information in your *Theology* books, *Commentaries*, *Word books* and *Bible Dictionaries*, in order to see broader perspectives surrounding your passage of scripture. Be sure to record pertinent information in your personal notes for future references.

COMPARITIVE ANALYSIS OF SCRIPTURES

Now that you have developed *exegetical*, and *hermeneutical* notes (*literary context, historical-social context & theological, wordbook, and dictionary notes, based upon the world of the text, and the larger world behind the text that informs your passage of scripture*), we are now ready to proceed to performing a comparative analysis of your passage of scripture, based upon the accumulation of information recorded in your personal notation documents that were retained for future references. Ask yourself the following questions, before comparing your documents:

> What do I now know, about the meaning of my passage of scripture, that I did not know before?

> What questions do I have about the text, that still have to be answered?

Keep your answers to both of these questions in the back of your brain as we proceed. As you compare your exegetical, form-literary, historical-social, commentary, handbook, dictionary and theology notes, , in addition to what you believe the Holy Spirit is revealing to you about His intention for inspiring the penmanship of the author, how do you believe these streams of information complement each other? Is the Holy Spirit bearing witness with your final interpretation of your streams of information? Now document what you have come to believe was the message the author intended his audience to receive. Ask yourself the following questions again:

What do I now know, about the meaning of my passage of scripture, that I did not know before?

What questions do I have about the text, that still have to be answered?

Congratulate yourself for completing the basic *academics* for your **R**udiments **o**f **R**esearch activity.

Time to proceed to another important part of this process. After completing the *academics* of your **R**udiments **o**f **R**esearch activity, what words in your passage of scripture still appear to have eternal significance? Retain a copy of words with eternal significance for future references and review. You have just expanded your list of words with eternal implications and meanings. We will see later, how your list of eternal words, phrases, and meanings, may contribute to your progressive awareness of eternal realities in-Christ, within you.

DEVELOPING AN ATTITUDE FOR LIMITED APPLICATION

The *application* component of the **R**udiments **of** **R**esearch process involves establishing a connection between the activity of eternality, with your life, and lifestyle. Connection with eternality *evolves* from participation, to partnership, to companionship.

Participation occurs during your born-again experience, as you choose to follow the unction and promptings of the Spirit of Christ, within your spiritual soul on a daily basis.

Partnership, involves intentional planning, personal discipline, discipleship, responsibility, accountability, and answerability, regarding the daily decisions that advance the Kingdom of God in heaven, on earth.

Companionship, occurs during conscious awareness of our Oneness *in*, *of*, and *as*, representation, and replication of Divine Nature through Christ. Awareness of

Divine Oneness includes consciousness of the eternal Nature of God in heaven, within our spiritual Nature, in-Christ on earth. God's Nature is the same in eternal future, as well as the eternal now, therefore Divine Nature is timeless. Your personal awareness of the Divine Nature within your spiritual soul, equates to self-awareness that is timeless, and eternal. The desires within Divine Nature in heaven, now become the conscious desires within your spiritual Nature on earth. Oneness *with*, *in*, and *as* Christ, literally means that both you and Christ share the same Divine Nature of the Father in heaven, through the Spirit of Christ within you. In Oneness, your very existence is a mirror of the Divine Nature, Character and Persona of God, in-Christ. You have now become the *fullness* of what Adam initially was in the Garden of Eden, as the Image and Likeness of God (Yahweh-Elohim; Gen 2:7). Once again, as a *participant* with eternality, you simply learn how to obey and respond to intuitive spiritual unction of the Divine Nature of Christ within you. As a *partner* with the activity of eternality, your participation evolves from external obedience based upon doctrinal knowledge, to internalized conviction, self-control, and disciplined behavioral choices, in agreement with eternal activity, as a lifestyle. As a *companion* with the activity of eternality, you become conscious of the experience of Divine Oneness as you breathe in and out, daily, in addition to awareness of the power, presence and importance of "being" before behaving the Divine Nature of God, in-Christ. Whether you are a *participant*, *partner*, or *companion* with the activity of eternality in heaven, on earth, it is most important to know that all three stages evolve from the same Divine Nature of God. In the new world to come (new heaven and earth) , you will always exist *in*, *within*, and *as* the Divine Nature of God, in-Christ. Therefore, your in-Christ relationship, is actually the core-essence of your existence in the future, within your present now.

Components and elements of the eternality of God in heaven, on earth, requires identification at this time. What does eternality look like in heaven, on earth? Glad you asked. Some examples include the activity of the eternal Love of God, everlasting Peace, perpetual

Goodness of God, endless power of the Divine, enduring Righteousness of God, eternal words of Divine language, resurrection power of life over death, Divine Abundance, the Joy of the Lord, tranquility of Divine Presence, the atmosphere of Holiness in Worship, spiritual Awareness of God, and supernatural Faith with supernatural Works, all are just a few activities of the eternality of God in heaven, on earth. As we learn how to participate, partner, and companion with these eternal activities, we become a receptacle, that vehicles heaven's agenda for the eventual transformation of our present earth, into the new heaven on earth. You and I are the medium for the connection between the presence of God in heaven, and human presence in our world. The eternality of God's presence in the heavenly throne room, is the same eternality of presence, that God desires to inhabit all Kingdoms in our world (Matt 6:10; Rev 11:15). The eternal activity of God in heaven, is active in our present now, for everlasting outcomes and results. This is why it is so important for us to learn how to see eternality within the fabric of our scriptures through an *Eternal Lens*, as *consciousness* of eternality is required, before relationship with eternality can effectively affect change through us. The more, we are conscious of eternality, the better we align in agreement and lifestyle with the activity of eternality. Christ is eternal right now. As we are transformed into the Divine Nature of God by the eternal Spirit of Christ, we exist the eternality of Divine Nature in our spiritual soul, right now. This is why Jesus said, *"If anyone believes in me, he shall never die."* (John 11:26). If you plan on permanently living in Alaska, you begin learning about the territory, dialects, social customs, culture, dietary choices, weather, employment opportunities, and landscape, long before you move from your present location. The same logic applies, as we prepare for our eternal relationship with God beyond our present earth. We prepare by fully experiencing the eternality of God, in-Christ, as we exist in our present world.

We often disclose our desire to live for Christ, as our greatest passion. Do you not know that the meaning, message, and ministry of Christ, was eternal activity in heaven, on earth? As Christ was, and is, eternal, so was the essence of his ministry, message, and ultimate meaning of Messiahship, on earth. If we really want to witness and live for Christ in our world, let's begin by cultivating our relationship with the eternal activity of the Spirit of Christ. Let's intentionally learn how to see the activity of eternality in heaven, on earth, within us, and surrounding us, so that we can participate, partner, and companion fulfillment of Divine purpose for our lives. It is time to "be" the eternality of Christ that we spend so many hours learning about. The eternality of Divine *Life* within us, is our *Light* for the world to see (Matt 5:14). Our desire for eternality, our passion for eternality, our hope, and fulfillment in eternality, is what consumes us, as it did for Christ, our Savior.

LIMITED APPLICATION PROCESS

In previous paragraphs, the importance of _connection_ with the activity of eternality, was presented as the most essential component of the *application* process. It is the Will of God for the eternality of Divine activity in heaven, to also occur on earth, within you. This is why Jesus presented and released so many eternal realities in heaven, on earth, during his earthly ministry, from heaven. For example, Jesus informed earth of the words, language, and intentions of communication, based upon the Will of his Father, that originated from heaven. For example, "the words that *I speak are not my own, but of the Father, who dwells in me* (Jn 14:10), *I speak that which I have seen my Father do* (Jn 8:38), *I have given them your word* (John 17:14), *thy Will be done on earth as in heaven* (Matt 6:10), *Spirit of Truth shall speak what He hears* [from heaven] (Jn 16:13), *this commandment I have received from my Father* (Jn 10:18), *my words are living and life* (John 6:63), *as my Father has taught me, I speak these things* (John 6:10). These are but a few illustrations, that reveal the efforts of Christ to present the eternality of heavenly truths, realities, and expressions to our earth. As Christ introduced the presence of eternal realities in heaven on earth (Mark 1:15), he lived, died, and rose again, to fulfill the eternal agenda of God in heaven, in our world. Now if Christ thought it was important to share words from heaven with people on earth, then shouldn't we do the same? Building a library of words that reveal, infer, reference, and point towards the activity of eternality in heaven on earth, will certainly help in our efforts to speak eternally in our present ephemeral world. Since speaking from an authentic lifestyle is our most powerful platform for communication, it is imperative that we recognize the importance of application of the information that is received in our research of eternality. So, let's continue with the *Application* component of the **R**udiments **o**f **R**esearch process.

In your previous assignment, regarding the *Prospecting Process*, and limited *exegetical* and *hermeneutical* exercises, you were instructed to develop personal notes for future reference. Also, you asked to locate and document words within your passage of scripture that could possibly represent, imply, or refer to eternal meanings, thoughts, or activities. You were also asked to compile a list of words, that may implicate eternal possibilities for future considerations, as we evolve our vocabulary, eternally. Now we also need to ask the Spirit of Christ, Who is also the Spirit of Truth, to reveal how the words in your List of Eternal Vocabulary, can become a part of your daily communication with others.

Learning how to talk (ephemerally) as a child, was extremely important in order to communicate with your ephemeral world in a healthy manner. The same case applies, regarding our ability to learn how to talk eternally, in order to release the health of eternality into our world through our language and communication. Jesus said, *"my words are living, and they are life"* (Jn 6:63). The living words of Christ within us, are not empty, but embodied with the eternality of Christ's life. Intentionally speaking life into this world, is intentionally advancing the life of Christ' Kingdom over death in our universe. Our words become a healing balm, as well as a weapon against expressions of death in our world. We are determined to speak life with every breath that we have. This is why it is so important to look at scriptures through the *Lens of Eternality*, so that we can learn how to speak eternal words that emanate from the life of Christ and his Kingdom, into every situation filled with despair and destruction. We are the light, the salt, and vehicles of the language of life-eternal, in our world. Sin cannot speak to itself in a transformational way, only we can do that. If death is going to be transformed into life, then those who exist life, must speak life, in the midst of death in our world. Continue to develop your vocabulary list of words that represent the life of God, in-Christ. Build your list of words that focus on the activity of God's eternality in our world. We already know how to speak death, all too well. Like a child, it is time to re-learn how to speak all over again. This time our words, language, conversational intentions, vocabulary, presence, and communication of our very being, will express the eternality of God's Will in heaven, on earth. Our words are no longer pitiful, but powerful, no longer hellish, but healthy, and our intentions for communication are no longer based upon self-expression, but Divine expression through us. Time to Speak!

Examples of locating, the activity of eternality within the fabric of our scriptures, will be provided in the next chapter. The practice of extracting eternality from our scriptures, may be new for some of you. I am confident, that the more you practice this discipline, the more skillful you will become.

Now let's continue, by doing a *Step by Step* exercise together, engaging both *Prospecting* and **R**udiments **of** **R**esearch processes:

Let's begin the *Prospecting Process* as we look at John 1:1-5, (I prefer St. John because of its wealth of examples of eternality).

A. As I read the entirety of Chapters One, Two and Three in general, and verses 1-5 of Chapter One as my targeted text, my *Prospecting Process* awakened. An unction from the Spirit of God within me, sensitized me to eternal possibilities, that could be revealed through the following words in John 1:1-5: those words were as follows: *Beginning, Word, made, life, light,* and *darkness.* As I prayed over these words, I felt a confirmation within my heart, that exploration and research of these words in verses 1-5, would prove to be fruitful in my desire to locate realities of eternality in John 1:1-5. The words, denoted as "beginning, Word, made, life, light and darkness," would now constitute the outcome of engaging the *Prospecting Process* with the Holy Spirit, as well as my initial starting point for study. I was determined to know, what the Spirit of God within me, desired me to understand about the eternal meaning and relevance of these words, as verified through further study.

B. Having selected my six words through the *Prospecting Process*, I was now ready to engage **R**udiments **of R**esearch exercises. My exercise began with a comparison of John 1:1-5, from six different word-for-word bible translations. The New American Standard Bible (NASB), New Revised Standard

Version (NRSV), Revised Standard Version (RSV), New English Translation (NET), English Standard Version (ESV), and the New King James Version (NKJV), were the Greek and Hebrew word-for-word translations, that I used for side-by-side comparisons of John 1;1-5. During my Literary observations of this texts, I noticed that the text was written in an informational narrative (matter of fact) style, as if the author provided information to support a certain, and specific, point of view. I also noticed that the six words, that I selected during the *Prospecting Process*, were consistent in the same meaning, and definition, in each of the translations. This informed me that what I was reading, agreed with the work of the original author, and was precise. My Literary observations, evolved from cursive observation in the English text, to observation of John 1:1-5, in its original Greek language. I used

BlueLetterBible.org, which in the Interlinear section, provided the Greek words with corresponding Strong's Concordance reference Numbers, and pronunciation accent markings for each word used in John 1:1-5. My Interlinear research included information on the following English-Greek words in my *Prospecting Process* List; *"beginning"* (arche-G746), *Word* (Logos-G3056), *made* (Ginomai-G1096), *life* (Zoe-G2222), *light* (phos-G5457), *darkness* (scotia-G4653). I discovered that the actual Greek structure of the sentence in John 1:1 was slightly different than that of the English versions, as it ended with " *God was the word*," (in the Greek), rather than *the Word was God* in all English Translations. My Theological investigations, during my **R**udiments **of R**esearch process, helped me to understand why English grammar placed the subject before the object of the sentence, i.e., *word was God*, rather than the object before the subject, i.e. *God was the word*. This inversion of the subject before the object was equivalent to the common practice of object before the subject placement in the Greek language. Now the phrase, the "*Word was God*", made sense in the English translation, even though it was inverted in the original Greek.

C. I proceeded, during my **R**udiments **of R**esearch exercise, to look up the definition of each word in my *Thayer Interlinear* and *Strong's Concordance*, according to the location numbers, that were provided during my Interlinear research. The definition of the word " beginning" in my Thayer Interlinear included the absolute beginning of all things. In the Strong's Concordance, the definition for the word beginning, included the following: "*beginning*" (arche-G746) is a feminine verb that denotes a singular event, person or thing , this word is pronounced as " Key" and comes from the Greek root word for etymology. The word "beginning," is used over 1,479 times in the bible and basically means a commencement, or order, time, place, first estate, power, principle, magistrate or rule. In John 1:1, the word beginning is used to denote primarily the origin of something, followed by the commencing of the first person in a series, the leader, the first place, principality, rule or magistracy. The results of my research on the word beginning, from the Thayer Interlinear and the Strong's Concordance, basically indicated the same information, relative to the initial, commencement, or first estate or existence of a person or a thing. In John 1:1, the beginning, referred to the presence of a persona, or person, within the existence of time. The implication is that the Word, existed before the existence of time, as well as within the existence of time. Therefore, time ultimately originates from the Word, and not vice-versa.

Then, I proceeded in my **R**udiments **of R**esearch process to understand the historical background behind the word (beginning) from the *Anchor Bible Dictionary, Interpreters Dictionary of the Bible and Supplementary Volume, and the Unger's Bible Dictionary,* in addition to reviewing professional assessments of what the "beginning" could mean in the Hebrew and Greek, as well as the inclusion of evolving Hebrew, B.C., meanings of the "beginning", within the A.D., meaning of Greek words. My conclusion was that in both Hebrew and Greek, the word for beginning, referred to the initiation of time in existence, that originated from Elohim (God/Hebrew), and Theos (God/Greek).

D. Now, I proceeded in my **R**udiments **of R**esearch process, to understanding the historical aspects of the world that informed the writer while penning his scripture. My *Bible Dictionary, Bible Handbook (Westermann, C. Handbook on the Old and New Testament) and The Harpers Atlas of the Bible* tools, helped me to understand how 1st century Hebrew communities, during which time the writings in this scripture were either written, collected, or orchestrated by whom many believe was the Apostle John, the influence of Platonism, had already modified many Jewish views of hell, heaven, possible immortality of the soul, distinctions between the soul and spirit, and understanding of eternality. Cultural influences during the time of the author, included the merging of philosophies regarding the existence of Spirit-beings before the existence of time, spirit-beings, existing in celestial time in the heavenlies and on earth as well. My study confirmed that the *beginning*, **referred to the pre-existence of the Word, Who was revealed as a spiritual Persona within the fabric of the creation of time in our universe**. My notations, and documentations on the Historical and Theological part of my research, concluded the *Academics*, of my **R**udiments **of R**esearch.

E. Now I needed to engage the Personal *Application* process of my **R**udiments **of R**esearch activity on the meaning of "beginning." I asked the Holy Spirit, to open the *"eyes of my understanding,"* regarding the relevance of the "beginning" to eternality in my scripture. Through prayer, I understood that the "beginning," is a continuation in the narrative of the existence of God before the creation of the existence of time. Whatever is eternal, exist before, as well as within and beyond the creation of time. Therefore, the "beginning," in John 1, was simply a continuation of the existence of eternality, that was present before the creation of the beginning of time. Because of eternality, the creation of the "beginning " of time was possible. Remember, eternality, is present, before the existence of time, and eternality, serves as the ultimate sustainer of all that exist, within the creation of time. Final conclusion: the existence of the *"beginning,"* originated from the eternality of God, Who exist, before the creation of the existence of time, in our universe. In short, <u>because of eternality, the existence of a *beginning* for time in our universe, was possible.</u>

F. *Personal application*: the eternality, in-Christ, within me, existed before the creation of time in our universe. Since eternality, exist before creation, and is therefore uncreated, there is the presence of the uncreated Divine Nature of God within me, in-Christ. This uncreated presence of the Divine, existed before the creation of time, and will continue to exist within me, beyond the culmination of time. In short, there is a part of my personhood in-Christ, that is timely, and timeless. I am learning how to grow in awareness of the timeless aspects of my personhood, in-Christ, in preparation for an everlasting relationship with God, in His eternal society, in my future.

G. **SUMMARY:** **R**udiments **of** **R**esearch: _Academic_ Conclusion for the *"beginning."* In John 1:1, the beginning equates to the presence of the pre-existing Word, within the initial creation of the creation of time, in our universe, before the creation of anything else.

H. **SUMMARY:** **R**udiments **of** **R**esearch: *Application* Conclusion for " beginning." The uncreated Divine Nature of the Word of God, exist in-Christ, within me. That means there are realities of God, in-Christ, that are inherent in my identity, that pre-exist the creation of time, and will exceed the culmination of time. In-Short, the eternality, of God, in-Christ, is also eternality, within the core of my spiritual soul, as well. I am an eternal being, whose spiritual existence originated from God, beyond time, and I will consciously continue to grow in Divine awareness, through time. It takes the eternal to desire the eternal. This is why the appetite of the eternal Nature of God, in-Christ, within me, desires the eternality of God, in time, through time, and beyond the beginning of the existence of time in our universe.

Both my *Academic* **R**udiments **o**f **R**esearch and my *Application* of **R**udiments **o**f **R**esearch, have been illustrated (in a limited form), as a Model for the development of your own structure for **R**udiments **o**f **R**esearch exercises. I only focused on the word *"beginning"* as an example for this book. Of course, my research included all six words that were on my *Prospecting Process* List. It would simply take too long for me to include all of the information, gathered from my *Academic* and *Application*, **R**udiments **o**f **R**esearch studies, for inclusion in this book.

The next chapter will provide some examples of the wealth of eternality, that is hidden within the fabric of scriptures in the Gospel of John.

CHAPTER FOUR

ETERNALITY EXAMPLES IN THE GOSPEL OF ST. JOHN

Plenty of episodes in our scriptures that conceal eternal truths, await discovery by those who desire to look deep enough to find them. The Gospel of John, is replete with disclosures of eternality in almost every chapter. I did some digging for you in order to provide examples of timeless activities and truths such as, eternal presence, thoughts, words, and language from our eternal Father that were revealed, and released, by Jesus on this planet. Revelations of eternal love, peace, mercy, forgiveness, resurrection power, as well as episodes of direct communication between our Father in heaven and our eternal Christ, on earth, have been highlighted.

My disclosures of eternality in the Gospel of John, are provided to just get you started. These disclosures are only a tip of the iceberg of what is available throughout the whole New Testament. Please feel free to formulate a List of Eternal **W**ords, **P**hrases, **T**houghts, **R**ealities, **P**owers, **A**ctivities, etc., as you review the information provided in this chapter.

LET'S BEGIN WITH THE GOSPEL OF ST. JOHN, CHAPTER SIX

During my research, I noticed that certain categories of eternal disclosures were consistently repeated in many chapters of the Gospel of St. John, so I developed *Category Labels* for these repeating disclosures of eternality. Under the Category of an eternal activity, reality, or presence, I indicated the location of the scripture, in addition to a brief explanation regarding the relevance of this scripture to an eternal reality.

After reviewing John, Chapter 6, from beginning to end, I discovered that the theme of *"everlasting life,"* dominated the context of activity throughout the chapter. As I engaged the *Process of Prospecting* I received an unction from the Spirit of God to focus on the words, *everlasting life,* from the very beginning of my study. While exercising the **R**udiments **of R**esearch, I discovered the Gospel of John, was originally written in the Greek language. The words for *everlasting life* in Greek are " A I O N I O S (everlasting)   ZOE (life)." Everlasting life is an expression of eternality, and therefore a desired treasure for you and me.   Certain realities, concerning the origination of Aionios Zoe in heaven and its availability, activity, and accessibility on earth, are disclosed in Chapter 6, as follows:

CATEGORY-1: ORIGIN OF EVERLASTING LIFE (AIONIOS ZOE)

The Source for the origination of Aionios Zoe:

John 6:57: Indicates the Father in heaven is the *Source* of everlasting life. [The source of everlasting life that resides within me comes from the eternal Spirit of God, through the Son, from the Father, in heaven].

Location for the origination of Aionios Zoe:

John 6:33,38,41,42,62: Indicates the heavenly origin for everlasting life. [the Eternal Everlasting Life in-Christ, within me, does not originate from earth, but from heaven. No institution of mankind can give me eternal life, and no institution of man can take it away because the eternality of eternal life originates from God. The ultimate experience of eternality, on earth, is initially in-Christ.]

Embodiment of Aionios Zoe:

John 6:47: Jesus Christ is the embodiment of heavenly Aionios Zoe, on earth. [Eternal, everlasting life, resides in-Christ. Therefore, eternality also resides, within me, in-Christ. The eternal realities of God, surrounding me, are also within me, in-Christ, i.e., Divine Love, Peace, Goodness, Life, etc.].

CATEGORY-2: REVELATIONS OF AIONIOS ZOE FROM HEAVEN ON EARTH

John 6:65:   Revealed the authorization for access of Aionios Zoe thru Christ. [Everything in the household of God in heaven or earth, functions under the Will of the Father, and is authorized by the Father, Rev 1:1; Matt 7:21]

John 6:11, 51:   Illustrated provisions, based upon Aionios Zoe laws for heavenly life. [Jesus looked to heaven for heavenly multiplication, (*according to the heavenly laws of life*), to occur on earth, as he looked to heaven while blessing provisions, before distributing them]

John 6:20,21:   Illustrated travel, based upon heavenly laws of physics that govern activity in the eternality of Aionios Zoe life. [Physics, under the Laws of Life, can be instantaneous, and are simply different from limited physics under the laws of Sin and Death: Rom 8:2]

John 6:63, 68:   Revealed   eternal   communication, based upon the realities of Aionios Zoe (everlasting life). [Words of Life are living words that reside under the Laws for Life, in-Christ, and the Kingdom of God (Rom 8:2)].

My examples of eternality in John 6, will end here. I am sure you will discover more while conducting your own **R**udiments **o**f **R**esearch studies. You are encouraged to enter the words *"everlasting life* (Aionios Zoe), into your *List of Eternality Expressions in the Scriptures* for future reference and consideration. Every one of my personal commentaries, provided in John 6, either revealed, implied, or expressed, some form of eternality that embodies everlasting life. Again, everlasting life, in-Christ, is also within you and me, because of our in-Christ union and relationship. So it is incumbent upon us to pray for revelation and wisdom, as to how we can partner, participate, or companion, with the presence and activity of everlasting life, that is available to us in the here and now, in-Christ.

A review of eternality in St John , Chapter 7, is provided below:

CATEGORY-1: CHARACTERISTICS OF EVERLASTING PARTNERSHIP

FLOWING, WITH TIMING IN HEAVENLY ETERNALITY:

- John 7:8, 30:   An example of action on earth, based upon authorized timing, in heaven. [Events in John 7 occurred according to heaven's timetable for the ministry, death, and resurrection of Christ on earth]. All activities, in the heavenly household are authorized by God before initiation. The Will of God for His heavenly household, is also the same Will for his household on earth (Matt 6:10).

- John 7:10:   Jesus concealed kingdom revelation until authorized by the Father to release it. [Jesus waited, until the appropriate time and place were in sync, with the Will of the Father in heaven, before disclosing heavenly truths, on earth].

- John 7:14:   Jesus revealed the Kingdom in agreement with heavenly timing & protection. [Another example of the eternality of Kingdom activity on earth, based upon Throne room authorization, in heaven].

CONDUITING ETERNAL COMMUNICATION IN HEAVEN, ON EARTH

- John 7:16:   Provides an illustration of Doctrine, that is equivalent to concepts, words, intentions, principles, revealed and released to earth, from the eternal Father in heaven, thru Christ.

- John 7:6,8, 29:   Interaction, based upon Divine Authorization is always the governing principle of our eternal Father in heaven. [Once again, we are reminded that occurrences within the household of God in heaven or earth, occur as authorized by the Father in heaven]. Theme: Household happenings, occur per authorization from the Father in the Throne room.   .

- John 7:17: Jesus introduced an eternal Logic Model for heavenly interaction on earth, as follows: "<u>OF</u>" God always *agrees* with "<u>OF</u>" God. [God has no problem consistently agreeing with Himself, in heaven, or earth]

- John 7: 37-39: An e*xample* of Spirit to spirit vocabulary & heavenly provisions. [An obvious example of Jesus speaking to the spiritual souls of his audience about spiritual provisions, that result in everlasting fulfillment]

My examples of eternality in John 7, will conclude here. My wife and I did discover many more in this chapter, and I hope you will also during your **R**udiments **o**f **R**esearch exercises. Again, praying for insight and revelation, as to how these scriptures in John 7, can increase your awareness of eternality within and around you, is my prayer for you.

Jewels of eternality in John, 8 are provided below:

CATEGORY-1: ETERNAL COMMUNICATION FROM HEAVEN TO EARTH

- *HEAVENLY COMMUNICATION:*

    - John 8:23,42,58: Communication, that originated from eternal beings in heaven, interacts with earth. [Jesus reveals, the eternality of his spiritual identity, and communication, that originated from heaven].

    - John 8:17-18: Jesus offers an interpretation of the Law of Moses thru a heavenly view of life over death (Rom 8:2). [This heavenly interpretation of Lawful validation of truth, could only be understood from a heavenly perspective].

    - John 8:19, 42: Jesus revealed the *eternality of Oneness,* from a heavenly perspective. [The Divine Nature of the Father, is also in the Son, and also within us, thru the

Son). Jewish culture had no clue of this kind of Oneness.

- John 8:20: The eternality of Jesus, reveals awareness of heavenly timing and protection on earth. [Movement on earth, in sync with the Will of the Father in heaven]

- John 8:26: An illustration, of Jesus conduiting language from the eternal Father in heaven to earth. [Jesus reveals again that the eternality of his language for communication on earth, originates from the eternal Father in heaven].

HEAVENLY BEHAVIOR:

- John 8: 28,29,38,40: An illustration of eternal proclivities of behavior in heaven on earth, through the example of Christ.

- John 8:12: An example of eternal identity, through an *Eternal Lens* is provided. [*Light*, equals eternal *Life*: John 1:4. This means that the presence of eternal life within us *in* this world, is the *Light* of God's eternal *Life to* this world of darkness]

- John 8:31,32: An example of eternal Truth is provided. [The eternal Spirit of Truth reveals eternal truths from heaven to earth, for disclosure of eternal truth <u>in</u> heaven, <u>on</u> earth; John 15:26; 16:13]

My examples of eternality in John 8, will end here. I trust you will discover more treasures of eternality in Chapter 8 through your own **R**udiments **of R**esearch exercises. This was truly a chapter that was rich and ripe with a wealth of eternality in heaven, on earth.

Examples of eternality in John, Chapter 9 are provided below:

CATEGORIY-1: ETERNAL TIMING FOR MANIFESTATIONS ON EARTH

John 9: 3,4:   The episode of death, was understood as an episode of opportunity regarding demonstration of the eternality of resurrection power, in-Christ, according to heaven's timetable.

John 9:5:   An illustration of heavenly timing, regarding the revelation of the Light of Eternal Life on earth, is provided.

John 9: 7-9:   Eternality, is illustrated, through the healing power of our eternal God that gave the blind man a new awareness of identity.

My examples of eternality in John 9, will end here. I hope you will discover more treasures of eternality during your study and research of this chapter.

Examples of eternality in Chapter 10, are provided below:

John 10:7-9: The new presence of God is no longer limited to the Holy of Holies in the Temple (*The Ark of the Covenant, in the Holy of Holies section of the Temple had been removed during the Babylonian invasion of 587-586 B.C., and had not been returned, therefore the Ark of the Covenant, that God honored with His actual presence, was actually missing in the Holy of Holies section of the Temple during the time of Christ*), The new connection, between God and Man, now occurred through the person of Jesus, the Christ, as the new *spiritual* Ark of the Covenant, according to God's eternal agenda in heaven, on earth.

John 10:9, 10, 14,-16, 22,23: The new connection between God in heaven, and man on earth, was no longer limited to rituals in the Holy of Holies, but with the presence of Jesus at Solomon's porch (global Court of the Gentiles & Women), located in the universal section of the Temple. The Holy of Holy was reserved, only for Jewish priest. However, the Court of the Gentiles was available to every soul. According to the agenda of our eternal God in heaven, Jesus would not be found in the Holy of Holies, or

Priest or Jewish men only compartments of the Temple, but at the place in the Temple, where <u>all</u> humanity could have an opportunity to experience God, through Christ.

CATEGORY-2: COMMUNICATION FROM ETERNAL BEINGS IN HEAVEN, ON EARTH

- John 10: 17-18: An illustration of *Resurrection Language*, directly received from the Father in heaven, is provided. (Earth had no clue of what Jesus was saying).

- John 10: 29: The Believer's everlasting relationship is appointed and guaranteed by the eternal Father in heaven.

CATEGORY-3: RULING PROPENSITY OF DIVINE NATURE

- John 10:25, 30: The eternal works of Christ, verified his ONENESS in heaven with our eternal Father. [Eternal relationship between God, the Father and Son, manifested on earth].

- John 10:34:   "Ye are gods" (Elohim = Rulers Psalms 82:6). Adam, as the Image and Likeness of God, represented the highest ruling revelation of God (in heaven) on earth in the Garden of Eden.

- John 10:36:   Now Jesus declares himself as the Son of God, (in reference to verses 34-35), which means Jesus (not Adamic Ruler-Elohim) is now the highest ruling revelation of God (in heaven), on earth.

Note:

The ruling propensities of the eternal Divine Nature that was in Adam/Eve and Jesus Christ (Jn 10:34-36) , are also within you, and me, in-Christ.

My examples of eternality in John 10 will end here. There are more hidden jewels of eternality in this chapter. You are encouraged to continue to search and pursue the treasures of eternality in this chapter during your **R**udiments **of R**esearch exercises.

Examples of eternality in John 11, are provided below:

CATEGORY-1: ETERNAL COMMUNICATION FROM HEAVEN TO EARTH

- John 11:42:   This episode, revealed direct eternal Father-to-eternal Son communication from heaven to earth. [Example of eternality in heaven, illustrated on earth, big time].

CATEGORY -2: ETERNALITY OF KINGDOM AUTHORITY IN HEAVEN, ON EARTH

- John 11: 43:   An illustration of heavenly authority of resurrection power over death, on earth

My examples of eternality in John 11, will conclude here. I trust you will discover more relevant clues of eternality in John 11, through your own **R**udiments **of** **R**esearch exercise.

Examples of eternality in John 12, are provided below:

CATEGORY-1: ETERNAL LIFE IN HEAVEN, ON EARTH

John 12:25:   Eternal life, in-Christ,   is accessible through Jesus Christ, the *Son of Man* (Jn 12:23; Dan 7:13)

CATEGORY-2: ETERNALITY EXEMPLIFIED THROUGH DIRECT COMMUNICATION WITH THE FATHER IN HEAVEN:

John 12: 27-30:   Jesus talks directly to the eternal Father in heaven, followed by the eternality of 'God's voice in heaven, talking directly to Jesus, and also the crowd of people. [Big time eternality example].

CATEGORY- 3: EXAMPLE OF ETERNAL AUTHORITY IN HEAVEN, ON EARTH

John 12: 49-50:   An illustration of behavioral activity, based upon prior authorization from the eternal Father in heaven, is provided.

My examples of eternality in John 12, will end here. There are more hidden jewels of eternality in this chapter, just waiting for discovery as you conduct your **R**udiment **of R**esearch exercises.

Examples of eternality in John 13, are provided below:

CATEGORY-1: ETERNALITY, SEEN THROUGH HEAVENLY TIMING, ON EARTH

John 13:18:   The Supper occurred at the appropriate time for fulfillment of scriptures, that were written over 700 years before this event (Psalms 41:9).

John 13:27:   Jesus confirmed that the <u>time</u> for the betrayal by Judas, had arrived.

John 13: 31:   Jesus illustrated his awareness of ordained activities in the eternality of time on earth, as he indicated that his <u>time</u> for death had arrived as an opportunity for glorification, from a <u>heavenly</u> <u>point of view</u>. Earth (Jewish culture) had no clue of the concept of crucifixion as a victory over death for their Messiah.

CATEGORY -2: CHARACTERISTICS OF ETERNAL RELATIONSHIPS IN THE KINGDOM

John 13:3-5:   Jesus, while possessing all heavenly authority, demonstrates the strength of his authority on earth through humility, and service that redeems, and values others. [This is how authority is exercised in the heavenly household].

John 13: 14-17:   We are to follow the example of Jesus in demonstrating heavenly exercises of eternal authority on earth, thru humility, and service, that actively venerates human value ("servant"-service) and is redemptive ("clean" & cleansing) for others.

John 13: 20:   Receiving the disciples of Jesus, is equivalent to receiving Jesus, himself, and is also equivalent to receiving the Father in heaven. [This eternal concept of integral Oneness, can only be revealed from a heavenly perspective by the eternal Spirit of Christ].

CATEGORY- 3: ETERNAL COMMANDMENTS IN HEAVEN, ON EARTH

John 13: 34-35:   Jesus, who <u>originates</u> from heaven (in spiritual soul), releases heavenly commandments on earth.

My examples of eternality in John 13, will end here. Please be encouraged to locate more examples of eternality in this chapter during your **R**udiments **of R**esearch exercises.

Examples of eternality in John 14, are provided below:

CATEGORY-1: ETERNALITY INCLUDES HEAVENLY REAL ESTATE:

- John 14: 2-a: Revelation of the inclusion of Heavenly Mansions, as our inheritance of heavenly estates, forever, is provided. [example of physical structures of heavenly provisions, in eternality, is revealed, on earth, by Christ].

CATEGORY-2: EXAMPLES OF ETERNAL ONENESS IN HEAVEN, ON EARTH

EXAMPLE OF ONENESS IN HEAVEN ON EARTH

- John 14: 9:   Jesus is the face of the Father in heaven (Jn 1:18-NIV; Jn 14:6; Col 2:9). God, Who exist beyond the existence of creation, reveals himself within creation through Christ.

- John 14:10:   I AM in the Father = Throne room Oneness. [As the Father refers to Himself as the I AM, so does the Son, as both are of the same Divine Nature]

  - John 14:11:   The works of the Father thru Jesus, verify Oneness. [*The same Divine Nature of the Father in heaven, within the Son, are verified through the eternal activities of the Father, thru the Son, on earth*]. The miraculous activities of Christ, verify the Divine Nature of the Father, within Christ, as well as the Divine Nature of the Father actualizing the miracles of Christ through the power of His Spirit.

- John 14:12:   Jesus is the *revelation* of the *replication* (not just the representation) of Oneness in heaven on earth. This means that Jesus is the authentic experience of Oneness with the Father in heaven. This also means, that in-Christ, we exist in the Oneness of Divine Nature, that permeates the heavenly household, eternally. *We need growth in awareness of our Oneness in God, in-Christ.* The Oneness of God, within His Divine Nature, is the Unity of the Body of Christ within the Nature of God. We are already One, we just need awareness of it, rather than awareness of our cultural disunities.

- John 14:19:   Eternal life, expressed AS your life, is a state of "being" , before the possession of "having."

- John 14:20:   We (Body of Christ) are "that day" of witnessing In-Christ as the Oneness of God in heaven, on earth.

CATEGORY-3: ETERNALITY IN HEAVEN INCLUDES RESOURCES

PROCUREMENT OF HEAVENLY RESOURCES: EXAMPLE

- John 14:13,14: "en"(G-#1722) same preposition used in 14: 2,10,11, and equates to "WITHIN" in English) this contextually means to ask **within my name.** The preposition, indicates ownership, relative to the relationship between both *subject* and *object* of the preposition. What this means is that we are authorized to ask for what has already been provided by the Father *within* the *person,* of the *name,* of Jesus Christ. We have not been authorized to ask for things, outside of what is within the person, of the name, of Jesus. God has not obligated Himself, to fulfill solicitations, outside, or beyond, of what is within the *person* of the *name* of Jesus Christ. Stop asking for things that are not in- Christ, or that Christ is not in. Realities, that are *in, of,* and *as* Christ, have already been provided, and can be procured, upon our solicitation to the Father, in the name of the Son. Example, we never ask God to bless us with Sin, because it does not exist within the person, of the name, of Jesus. However, we can ask for greater awareness of the eternality of Divine Joy because it exist, within the person, of the name, of Jesus. As we ask, we receive, because our request has already been authorized, and approved, by the Father in heaven, for access on earth, in-Christ.

CATEGORY- 4: ETERNALITY INCLUDES EVERLASTING SECURITY

EXAMPLE OF HEAVENLY SECURITY

John 14: 16: *"Forever,"* indicates the permanent presence of the eternality of Divine Nature, **with** us. [eternal companionship revealed]

John 14: 17: *"Spirit from heaven with, and* **within** *us."* (expansion of Vs 16, regarding companionship with the eternal Spirit of God, from *with*, to eternally *within* us, forever) [eternality revealed big time].

John 14: 18:   Christ's return from heaven, as assurance of promises on earth, fulfilled from heaven.

John 14: 19:   *"Because I live, you will live also,"* is another assurance that the eternality of life, in-Christ, is also the eternality of life in the Body of Christ.

CATEGORY- 5: ETERNALITY IN HEAVEN INCLUDES REWARD FOR OBEDIENCE

EXAMPLE OF HEAVENLY OBEDIENCE

John 14: 15:   Obedience is both the standard for aptitude, and attitude in the heavenly household of God, as illustrated by heavenly Angels (Psalms 103:20). [Divine obedience, is an imperative for all inhabitants in the household of God in heaven, or earth]

John 14: 21,23: Obedience = Reward of greater Awareness that also equals Eternal Growth. [*Divine Awareness is growth, and growth is Divine Awareness, for inhabitants, within the household of God in heaven or earth. In the heavenly Throne room, one's station, in proximity and closeness to the seat of the Father in the Throne room, indicated the degree of Divine Awareness, that was possessed*]. Maturity, in the Throne room, is indicated by degrees of Divine Awareness. Example: The Beast, which was full of eyes in front and back (awareness of God), in addition to 24 Elders, were stationed in close proximity to the throne room seat of the Father as an indication of exemplary Divine awareness, whereas other celestial beings, were stationed further away from the Father's seat in the Throne room (Rev 4:7-9; 5:11-13).

CATEGORY – 6: THE ETERNALITY OF DIVINE
TRUTH

EXAMPLE OF HEAVENLY TRUTH

John 14: 6:   *"I AM, the Way, the Truth, and the Life."* Relationship with the eternal person of Jesus Christ, is required for everlasting relationship with the eternal Father. [Relationship with Yeshua (Son), required for relationship with Yahweh (Father)]

John 14: 7:   As Jesus is the Divine Nature of God in heaven on earth, so is he the face of the Father in heaven, on earth.

John 14: 26:   We will be taught from heaven," *to* earth, by the Spirit of Christ from heaven, *on* earth. [Example of Throne room eternality, revealed through the heavenly teachings of Truth, through the Spirit of Truth from heaven.]

John 14: 27:   Eternal peace is given & sustained from heaven on earth by Jesus Christ.

John 14: 28a: *Messiah's departure from earth*: Messianic *departure* and *return*, was the introduction of a non-traditional, new doctrine, that was antithetical to historical traditions regarding the _permanent_ presence, rule, and reign of the Jewish Messiah over the Gentiles. [Jesus introduced a concept (leaving and returning to earth) that Jewish tradition and earth, had no concept of, only eternal beings in heaven were aware of the concept of the Messiah's departure and return from heaven, as a phase of Kingdom rule].

28b: The Divine Father, *as greater than the son of man*, was congruent with John 13:16, where Jesus defines his role on earth, as a Servant. [The Role of Jesus, on earth, as a servant and the son of man, is inferior to his eternal Role at the right hand of the Father in heaven as the Lamb and Son of God].

CATEGORY -7: ETERNALITY INCLUDES HEAVENLY LANGUAGE

EXAMPLE OF HEAVENLY LANGUAGE ON EARTH

- John 14: 10:   Christ confirms the origin of his vocabulary on earth as the vocabulary of his Father in heaven. [Episode of eternal vocabulary from our eternal Father in heaven, revealed thru Christ on earth].

- John 14: 24:   Revelation of the eternal Father's vocabulary in heaven, on our earth, by Christ. [Example of a continuation of John 14:10].

This concludes my examples of eternality in John 14.

You are encouraged to do your **Rudiments of Research** on this chapter for the discovery of more golden nuggets of eternality, that are hidden within the fabric of scriptures, in this chapter.

Now, I am going to provide just Categorical examples of eternality within several chapters of St. John, in order to provide opportunities for you to complete these Categories through your **Rudiments of Research** exercises. Determine the appropriate reasons why each scripture was placed under its respective categorical heading.

Examples of eternality in John 15 are provided below:

HEAVENLY ONENESS	ACCESS HEAVENLY RESOURCES	HEAVENLY RELATIONSHIPS
Jn 15: 4,5,9,10,11	Jn 15: 7,8,16	Jn 15: 12,13,15,17,19
HEAVENLY INSIGHTS	HEAVENY WITNESS OF JESUS	HEAVENLY JUDGEMENT
Jn 15: 1,2,3,26	Jn 15: 26,27	Jn 15: 25

Your assignment is to determine why the scriptures, above, were placed under their respective category as it relates to eternality.

Examples of eternality in John 16 are provided below:

- HEAVENLY ONENESS   ACCESS HEAVENLY RESOURCES HEAVENLY PROPHETIC

- 27, 28 Jesus in/of Father   23, 24 Ask-thru person of name 2,3,4 – Pre-event
  disclosure

- HEAVENLY INSIGHTS HEAVENY IMPARTATION HEAVENLY JUDGEMENT

- 5,7,8-9,15,16,20,22   13: H-Truth into earth   9,10: Divine Righteousness exist

Again, your assignment is to determine why the scriptures, above, were placed under their respective category as it relates to eternality.

My examples of eternality for Chapter 16, will end here. Please take the time to determine why the scriptures were placed under their Categories.

My examples of eternality in John 17, are provided below:

HEAVENLY AUTHORITY

Jn 17: 3, 6, 8, 18

HEAVENLY INSIGHT-AWARENESS

Jn 17: 3-5, 7-10, 12,14, 15, 16,19,24,25

HEAVENLY ONENESS

Jn 17: 10,11,21-23, 26

HEAVENLY PROPHETIC

Jn 17: 11,13,17,20,24,25

HEAVENLY MULTIPLICATION

Jn 17: 20,21,23

HEAVENLY MANIFESTATION

Jn 17: 1,4,5,6,8,13,14,17,18,22,26

- **HEAVENLY TIMING**

Jn 17: 1

HEAVENLY FULFILLMENT

Jn 17: 12

My examples of eternality for Chapter 17, will end here. Please take the time to determine why the scriptures above were placed under their Categories.

My examples of eternality in John 18, are provided below:

John 18: 6: Eternality of power in Heaven, demonstratively confirming the heavenly meaning of " I AM, HE," on earth.

John 18: 11: Jesus confirms meaning of this event through eternal Eyes of the Father in heaven. [Example of *Seeing* events on earth, thru an Eternal Lens in heaven].

John 18: 36-37: Jesus discloses the meaning of the eternality of TRUTH, from a heavenly point of view.

My examples of eternality for Chapter 18, will end here. Please take the time to explore and discover more gems of eternality in this chapter.

My examples of eternality in John 19, are provided below:

SCRIPTURES, <u>ORIGINATED</u> THRU HEAVENLY SPIRIT, ARE <u>FULFILLED</u> ON EARTH:

John 19: 1,3:
< See Isa 50:6 scourging>

John 19: 7:
<Lev 24:16 Lawful death by stoning>
According to the Law, death for Christ should have occurred through stoning and not a crucifixion as instigated by the Rabbis and Chief Priest. However, Jesus knew that the *heavenly agenda* <u>required crucifixion</u> for his death, regardless of the criterion for death and punishment, mandated in the Law of Moses.

John 19: 23,24,28:
<Garment gambling>

< Psa. 22:18
Parting clothes & casting lots>

John 19: 33:
< Exo. 12:46; Ps 34:20 No broken bones>

John 19: 37:
< Zech. 12:10 Piercing spear>

John 19: 41,42:
< Isa 53:9 Wicked thieves & Rich man tomb>

My examples of eternality for Chapter 19, will end here. Please take the time to determine why the scriptures above were placed under their respective Categories.

My examples of eternality in John 20, are provided below:

- **KINGDOM OF HEAVEN MANIFESTATIONS:**

- John 20: 1   Evidence of eternal beings in heaven, manifested (made visible) on earth. Stone Rolled away (by an Angel from Heaven: (See Matt 28:2 for event behind the story).

- John 20:12   Evidence of eternal beings in heaven, manifested (made visible) on earth, again. Two speaking Angels inhabited the tomb (head and foot of resurrection bed). [Two eternal beings, from heaven, conveyed information of eternal significance, to women on earth.

- John 20:17   Jesus, in an ascending body, resurrected by the eternality of power in heaven, communicates his intentions with Mary.

- John 20: 17   Jesus, in a resurrected body for future Christians, provided directives which told Mary where to go and what to say upon arrival.

- John 20:19   Jesus, in a resurrected body for future Christians, enters the room thru walls/doors. This reveals that eternality, in the ascending body of Jesus and future body of Christians, is not limited to our present laws of physics on earth but can transcend them.

- **KINGDOM OF HEAVEN MANIFESTATIONS, CONTINUED...**

- John 20:20, 27   The eternal, resurrected body of Jesus, retained some observable forms of his previous body, i.e., wounds in hands and side.

- John 20:19,21,26   Jesus changes the atmosphere from ephemeral fear, to heavenly peace, as he released the eternality of peace from heaven, into a room full of human fear. [Activity of eternal peace, on earth].

- **KINGDOM OF HEAVEN REALITIES ARE REVEALED:**

- John 20:9   Scriptural promises, concerning the resurrection, were being fulfilled from heaven's perspective even though earth did not have a clue.

- John 20: 17   The resurrected Jesus, *selected, authorized,* and *commissioned,* a female to be the first to deliver the Resurrection Gospel to others.

- John 20: 21   The resurrected Jesus, *selected, authorized,* and *commissioned* men to share with the world.

- John 20: 22   The resurrected Jesus prophetically breathes the anointing of the Spirit from heaven upon his disciples. [Anointing UPON, is always for supernatural power].

- John 20: 23   The resurrected Jesus prophetically authorizes disciples to exercise the eternality of heavenly authority over sin, on earth

- **KINGDOM OF HEAVEN EPISODAL LESSONS:**

- John 20: 29   Blessings, by our eternal Christ upon Believers, who have not seen, nor touched the resurrected body of Jesus.

- John 20: 30-31   The resurrection narrative was generationally written for future believers to receive the eternality of life, in-Christ, through faith.

My examples of eternality for Chapter 20, will end here. Please take the time to conduct further research on the additional rich deposits of eternality that are hidden in this chapter.

My examples of eternality in John 21, are provided below:

- **KINGDOM OF HEAVEN <u>PROPHETIC</u>:**

- John 21: 6.   Foreshadow of the disciples of Jesus, as fishermen, becoming fishers of men, through the ministry of the resurrected Christ. [The ministry of Christ would produce salvation, as an everlasting outcome of eternal significance].

- **KINGDOM REDEMPTION:**

- John 21: 6   Fish numbers represented the fruitfulness of ministry, restored through intervention of the resurrected Christ.

- **KINGDOM MANIFESTATION:**

John 21: 6   The spiritual exercise of eternal Faith, was physically manifested in the form of a multitude of fish.
[The Faith of God is eternal. The manifestation of this Faith as fish, provided an illustration of the Faith & Works of the Father in heaven, through Christ on earth].

- **KINGDOM AUTHORIZATION / COMMISSION**

- John 21: 15-17   Peter's mission and commission, was declared and authorized by our eternal Christ.

My examples of eternality for Chapter 21, will end here. Please take the time to locate and appropriate additional gems of eternality, that are resident in this chapter, awaiting your discovery!

CHAPTER FIVE

BLESSINGS OF ETERNALTIY AWARENESS

I grew up in a mainline evangelical Christian church. Sunday School provided the foundation for most of my Christian education. Sunday sermons provided motivation to accept Jesus Christ as my Lord and Savior, and to live a godly lifestyle. I was reminded every week of my need to repent for secret sins, in addition to choosing to love everybody as a way of pleasing God. I was told that I was responsible for *"working out my soul's salvation."* That meant that I had the responsibility of self-managing my sinful, fleshly urges through the daily discipline of reading the bible, devotional prayer, and active service of loving others, just as I loved myself. The highest level of Christian understanding that I received was the experience of being filled with the Spirit through spiritual baptism, and speaking in tongues as a means of experiencing a new power and presence of the Holy Spirit in my life, in addition to learning how to believe God for personal provisions, employment, career decisions, safety, a future spouse, and what college God wanted me to attend. This was an honest summary of my Christian growth. Many Christians that I knew, never even made it this far, as many fell back into former lifestyles of sin due to their inability to continue this ascetic lifestyle. I deeply appreciated all that the institutional Church provided throughout my many years of growth in Christ. Upon graduation from college, followed by graduation from Seminary with Bachelor and Master Degrees in various fields of Religion, respectively, I realized, as a religious professional, that I had more questions, than answers regarding my understanding of Christianity and the legitimacy of our interpretations of the bible. Seeing how Western theology scholars, reduced the truth of our great and infinite God to just Judeo-Christian perspectives, was mind-boggling for me. Apparently, God's pre-Jewish revelations of Himself to His non-Jewish families, (Gentiles), was irrelevant to the Jewish mind, and subsequently the Christian worldview also.

Understanding that Jews and Christians believed they were the only ones who righteously and legitimately knew our infinite God, caused problems for me. How could God be so small and so little, that words written about Him on scrolls, primarily from one race, could control the relationship of everyone else with Him on this planet? If God created all human beings, then humanity would be His family, not just the people who claimed to know God based upon a Hebrew bloodline, or writings on Jewish scrolls. Then there was the question of whose relationship with God was more powerful and righteous as I observed nations praying for God to help them destroy other nations. Can you imagine that? Praying to God for help to destroy God's own family? The Church's official and unofficial contributions to racism, classism, sexism, economic inequality, silence regarding the irresponsible destruction of our planet by corporations, development of atomic bombs, in addition to military spending to invent all sorts of weapons for the destruction of humanity, created great concerns in my mind regarding the presence, voice, complicity or silence of the Church in our society. I felt like there had to be more to Christianity, than what I was exposed to. Certainly, there had to be a deeper level that could be experienced in Christ. For me, Christianity had to be either above, or beyond the Sin problem of the world, but certainly not the problem, itself. Just as I was about to give up on Christianity as a realistic solution to the Sin problems of our world, God began opening my eyes to see beyond the temporary and ephemeral challenges of this life, and to see the presence of the eternality, that exist within the fabric of this life as its sustaining source. Since all existence originated from eternality, and is sustained through eternality, and will one day culminate eternally, then within Divine eternality, is the ultimatum of life, meaning, and the purpose for existence. Within eternality, we discover all everlasting truths and realities. Sin, and other ephemerality in this life, will perish and one day cease to exist in the presence of eternal truth. Only the things that are eternal are worthy of the majority of my time and attention. Eternal solutions and realities of God like eternal salvation, everlasting love, endless joy, and perpetual peace, are what I choose to participate with daily as fulfillment of purpose in this life.

Later, God revealed to me that the eternal is in the process of transforming the temporary, into the eternal. An example of this, is that our temporary societies are progressively being transformed into an eternal society, that will be ruled by Jesus Christ the heavenly Messiah on earth forever. As I was in the process of losing respect for the legitimacy of our bible, God opened my eyes to seeing the eternality of His presence, principles, and activity that was concealed within the fabric of our scriptures. Christianity became more than just a mental conception, or an opioid used to rule the masses by the elite, or even a fairytale hope to sustain us through the many trials of life, Christianity became an opportunity to see reality through a new lens, that being, an *Eternal Lens*. The scripture informed us that through the Holy Spirit, we would be able to see what *"eye hath not seen , nor ear has heard."* Now I know this to be empirically true. The Word of God informed us that *the "unseen is more real than what is seen."* As I am learning to see reality through the *Lens of Eternality*, I also concur that the unseen is greater and more authentic, than what we perceive with our five senses. I was taught how to study the bible scientifically and systematically from a scholarly perspective; however, it was really God, Who taught me how to see the realities of eternality that were often concealed within the fabric of the scriptures. As gold was under the ground in the Garden of Eden, and the treasures of the Kingdom of God were often hidden in the parables of Christ, great rewards await those who are willing to dig deep to find the treasures of eternality. I have learned that the wealth of eternality is worth our researching efforts to reveal its presence, and meaning, and message, for personal and global edification. I pray that everyone, who reads this book will be motivated to become seekers of eternality in our scriptures. Time is never lost but redeemed when invested in the eternality of God. Time is but a moment in eternity, therefore eternity lies within the essence of our daily experience of time. Relationship, in-Christ, is the redemption of time in eternity, and eternity in time. Time invested in God, is the best investment of your time in this life.

Avoidance of hell no longer consumes my energy. Awareness of eternal life, in-Christ, is the experience of my future, in my present now, therefore Christ is the major focus of my life, daily. Awareness of who I am, and becoming, in-Christ, is what I major on, and concerns about meeting the expectations of people or institutions is what I now minor on. *"For me to live is Christ."* Now I understand that Jesus Christ, is eternal, and in-Christ, so am I. Eternality is life-eternal. No longer will I equate Christianity to just the values and definitions of my present, ephemeral culture. Christ is eternal, the core-essence of Christianity is eternality, and through the *Lens of Eternality*, I will choose to see myself, and the people, who possess the Divine Nature of God, as His solution to the Sin problem of humanity in our world. Now I have shared enough about the personal resolves of my eternal journey, it is time to see how eternality can be of personal benefit in your life, and lifestyle.

If you only had several hours left to live, what would you prepare to take to heaven with you? What is of heavenly value in your life right now? This question, is not an absurd one, as it could possibly be your reality tomorrow. Shouldn't we major on preparation for the inevitabilities in this life? We are born to die. If born to die ends with a period, then was life really worth anything? However, if born to die is followed with a comma, then dying is only a pause to living again. Which ultimatum do you really desire, " born to die" or "born to live again, thru death?" Now consider how much time, and energy, and attention, you have devoted to daily preparation as an answer to both questions. Have your values, and the majority of your focus been upon things that will perish with death, or exist forever in heaven? Have you invested in participation, partnership, and companionship, with heavenly truths, manifestations, realities, and activities that occur daily on earth, or have we majored on the art of earthly survival for just earthly gain? Born to die or born to live again? How have you answered this question with your life, and lifestyle? You might think that this is a hard question to answer. I say, verification of your answer can be evaluated by the way you manage your time daily. How much time do you invest in participation, partnership, or companionship with heavenly interest, in opposed to earthly pursuits? Time, originates from God, therefore time belongs to Him.

How much of God's time do we offer back to him with our activities, thoughts, moments of heartfelt devotion, vocabulary, acts of godliness and love, times of heartfelt surrender, meditation, and visualization that is pleasing to the Divine? One of the definitions of "worship" is based upon what we consider as worthy of our time and attention. Does television, or the internet, command more of our time and attention as worship, than communication with our God? Can we take the internet or television to heaven with us? Can most of our thought-life enter into heaven with us? Will the majority of our activities on earth, continue in heaven? I think it is evident by now, that decisions have already been made, regarding our priorities in this world. The question is, how shall we remain after reading this chapter?

Our eternal God has not forsaken this earth but is eternally active in redeeming it. Why not join in with Him? This is what Jesus did. He looked to see the activity of His Father on earth, and simply joined in. As the Father worked, so did the son (Jn 5:19). Shouldn't we follow the example of Jesus by joining in with the redemptive, eternal work of the Father, through the Spirit of Christ on earth? The eternal activities of love, joy, peace, patience, mercy, righteousness, goodness, healing, eternal life, everlasting relationships, gentleness, knowledge, prosperity, wholeness, abundance, words of life, the faith-language of the Father, Son and Spirit in heaven on earth, is eternal because our God is eternal. Joining in, by participating, partnering, or companioning with the eternal work of our God, is joining in with God's redemptive solution for the Sin problem of mankind. As redemption for Sin, originated from our eternal God, to you and me, partnership with God, vehicles redemption for Sin through you and me. As God is the solution, through union with Him we also become the solution. People often wonder how they can help to make this world a better place. Joining in with the redemptive work of our eternal God is a decision that you can make daily. Your decision to join-in, is guaranteed to eternally affect a healthy change in this world, in addition to making a heavenly investment.

We know that our God is eternal. We also know that our eternal God is the ultimate author of the scriptures that were revealed to men by His Spirit. Why would our eternal God, place eternality within the fabric of our scriptures if He did not want us to discover it? Why have we been taught to only look for ephemeral, and temporary solutions for life's challenges in our bible, when our eternal God provided eternal solutions for this life and beyond? Seriously, who told us not to look for eternality in our scriptures, or better still, have you been searching, and researching the scriptures for eternality lately? Since our eternal God, desires an eternal relationship, with his eternal people, then shouldn't we be about the business of understanding the many realities of eternality right now? These are just straight forward questions that demand honest answers if we are to move forward. Should we keep using the bible to just learn how to live on this earth, or should we begin reading the bible to learn how to live through this earth, and beyond? Is the eternal activity of God, present on earth, as it is in heaven? Yes, it is! Was the meaning, message, and ministry of Jesus, based upon the eternality of God's Will in heaven? Yes, it was? Does the activity of Christ in this world through his Spirit, continue to advance the eternality of God's Will in this world? Yes! Apostle Paul told us to walk in the Spirit (Gal 5:25). Is walking in the eternal Spirit of God, also participating, partnering, and companioning, with the eternal work of God? Yes! Will you commit to the discipline of searching the scriptures, in order to discover **every** expression, inference, implication, revelation, and category of information, regarding the presence, activity, and availability of eternality, on earth? Your answer is _?

Association, results in assimilation. The more you are with a person, the more you are likely to become like that person. The more you participate, partner, and companion with the eternal work of the Spirit of Christ, the more you become the experience and expression of the eternality of the person of Christ in our world. Will you commit to becoming a vessel, receptacle, and vehicle for eternality in our world by cultivating an intimate relationship with the eternal Spirit of God? Your answer is _? Feel the pressure by now? Sometimes pressure is good for us when it comes to making serious decisions. Our world is dying. Sin is changing humanity into something that is less than human. Wars and disease, due to Sin, is taking an unprecedented toll on our future. We are killing our planet, just like we are killing ourselves. When will the killing end? You know, because you are God's solution, in-Christ. Every contribution that you make through participation with the redemptive work of the eternal Spirit of Christ, makes an everlasting difference to God. The Divine is counting on you, I am counting on you, unborn children are counting on you to prioritize an eternal lifestyle over an ephemeral lifestyle, in order to affect everlasting changes on this planet. We need you to join in! Be the difference. Be the solution. Allow your experience with the eternal, to also be the eternal expression of your life in your family, and in this world as well. The world needs to no longer see a religious Jesus, too many lives have been lost, and too many wars have erupted, because of a religious Jesus. The world really needs to see the *eternality* of Jesus, in heaven, on earth. The religious Jesus has been used to commercially make money to fulfill the unceasing lust of the rich during holiday seasons. The religious Jesus has been used to dehumanize our own brothers and sisters, based upon the color of the melanin in their skin, Jesus has been used for unjust political gain, Jesus has been used to justify the cruelest, most inhumane treatment of human beings in America through the institution of chattel slavery, that by the way, continues to be celebrated with Confederate flags to remind the descendants of slaves of how the oppressor, justifies oppression. Jesus has been used to justify killing our own children. Jesus has been used to justify the selfish accumulation of money and greed, rather than ministry to human need. Enough of exploiting Jesus Christ for fulfillment of mundane, earthly appetites that often occurs when a religious relationship with Christ reduces him to only that of ephemeral value rather than eternal appreciation. We need to see the *eternal value* of Jesus, daily, moment by moment, minute by minute, as a lifestyle, only then can we communicate the value of eternality with conviction in our world. Eternal sensitivity and awareness, begins *with* us, before it can effectively transform the world, *through* us. As you search the scriptures to discover the eternal deposits of God, know that the rewards of your discoveries are not just for you, but for this world also, through you. Your knowledge, eternal experiences through association and assimilation, and dedication to walking daily with the Spirit of God, is an investment that you can take directly into heaven, anytime, or any day. I reiterate once again, your investment into the eternality of Christ, is the wisest investment, you will ever make, whether you are financially wealthy or needy. We are all equals when it comes to the existential responsibility for deciding who or what we will invest our lives in. No one can decide for you or me. Investment of your time in conscious awareness of the eternality of God, in-Christ, is HIGHLY RECOMMENDED! Since eternality is in-Christ, within you, then investment, in-Christ, is also investment in yourself. In-Christ investments include everlasting, perpetual, endless and eternal rewards. Are you feeling like you are ready to *invest* more time in study of the Word of God through an *Eternal Lens*? Your answer is __?

Acceptance of God's Will concerning our life-purpose, will help our personal desires and dreams to align with Divine purposes, for the manifestation of solutions for Sin in heaven, on earth. Yeshua, the Christ, illustrated how personal desires can be in alignment with God's Will as he lived to reveal heavenly realities of wholeness over disease, freedom over demonic possession, relationship over religion, salvation over Sin, and the superiority of eternal life over eternal death through resurrection power. Following Jesus, is living the same lifestyle of eternality in heaven, on earth (See my following books: *Introduction to Eternal Living Now (1st book)* and *Eternal Living Now-Intermediate Level (2nd Book)*, for more information on heavenly realities, on earth.

W.W.J.D., is a common acronym for "what would Jesus do." In response to this question, Jesus demonstrated what he would do through his message and ministry during the first century, A.D. What did Jesus do?

He joined in with the eternal work of his Father in heaven, on earth. Again , I remind you, as we attempt to follow Christ, we must consciously, and intentionally, *join in* with the eternal work of the Father in heaven, through the Spirit of Christ, Who is affecting eternal outcomes, in, and through, our world? You are encouraged to develop a discipline of reading the scriptures through a *Lens of Eternality*, in order to see how to align with the eternal work of God on earth, daily. The time we have left on this earth, is all the time we need to affect redemptive change in our world. Investing in eternality, is a wise use of the time we have left. Changing W.W.J.D., to W.W.Y.D (What Will YOU Do?), is the real question to answer. Will we continue to focus on the ephemeral, for ephemeral outcomes, or do we now focus on the eternal, for eternal outcomes? Ephemerality equals cultural conformation, and eternality equals Kingdom transformation, which are you willing to invest in as a daily discipline? Which of these investments offer rewards that you can enter heaven with? Living for today, or living through today for tomorrow, is totally your choice. Choose wisely my friend. I chose eternality as my life, and lifestyle. The satisfaction and fulfillment I have received from making this choice, has been immeasurable. As a satisfied customer, I recommend the same choice for you also. Selah!

As aforementioned in this book, eternality, has probably been occurring around and within you all of the time. Growth in *awareness*, is required for us to effectively participate, partner, or companion, eternal activity in heaven, on earth. For example, awareness includes understanding that the experience of the presence of God, is an eternal experience. Experiencing the *inner-voice* of the Spirit of God, is an experience with the eternality of God, the presence of the Divine during worship, is an experience with the eternality of God, inspirations and revelations, received from the Spirit of Christ, are experiences with the eternality of God, spiritual insights and understandings that well-up in your spiritual soul while studying the scriptures, are moments of perceiving the scriptures through the *Lens* of our eternal Spirit, thus, it is an experience with the eternality of God. The moments we experience Divine peace in the midst of adversity, are also episodes of eternality, within and around us. Observing the eternal activity in our scriptures actualized in the daily activities of our lives, encourages us to connect with the Word of God both academically and empirically. Knowing, that the presence of eternality in the historical narratives of our scriptures, are yet present in our modern-day society, helps to establish greater relevance, regarding the eternal work of Christ, then, and now. Eternality is the Nature, and activity of God, in our past, present, and future experiences of Him in either heaven, or earth. The ultimate meaning of our lives, identities, and activities in-Christ, evolve from the eternality of Divine Nature. In-Christ, the Divine Nature of God becomes our history, future, and final evolution of our being. In short, eternality, is what God majors on, we are urged do the same.

For far too long, we have been informed about *what is not* of Christ, i.e., lust of the flesh, sinfulness, unlawful behaviors, wrong denomination as a cardinal sin, etc. It is time for us to see the eternality of God, in our scriptures, through an *Eternal Lens*, in order to share new information that majors on *what is eternal in our present Now,* in-Christ! The world-order is too occupied with itself and has no desire for focus on eternality. Religious culture, in my opinion, is often too occupied with maintaining its cultural status quo, and tends to focus too much on cultural survival in this world. If the eternal desires, intentions, purposes and Will of the Father in heaven, are to effectively be fulfilled in the eternal meaning, message, and ministry of our Christ, then you, and I, and all of the people, who are <u>OF</u> the Nature of God, must take on the responsibility of revealing the rich eternality of God in the scriptures to our world. Our God has an eternal message, and everlasting purpose for people who are, and will, experience an endless relationship with Him in this world and the world to come. *It takes the eternal to communicate the eternal.* This means, we cannot look to atheistic voices, or cultural religions, to vehicle eternality into our world. Communication of the eternality of God is our job, alone. In order to communicate the eternality of God effectively, we must know where to find it in our scriptures, and how to recognize it within our in-Christ experiences. We must be in command of language, that comprehensively informs others of what the eternality of life, heaven, Christ, Spirit of Christ, and the Body of Christ, really is. WE MUST DEVELOP OUR ETERNAL VOCABULARY SO THAT WE CAN SPEAK TRANSFORMATIVELY, rather than insecurely, in our world. We don't have to be afraid of other religious expressions of the ephemeral, when we understand how God is transforming the ephemeral into the eternal, and everlasting. The process of becoming the new heaven and earth has already begun. The initial announcement of the presence of the Kingdom of Heaven on earth (Mark 1:15), was also a revelation, that the process of the eternal, transforming the ephemeral, had already begun. Ready or not, the activity of eternality on our earth, will not cease until the Will of God in heaven, is fully activated and actualized, on earth, *as in heaven* (Matt 6:10). In-Christ, we are participants, partners, and companions, with the eternal activity of Divine Nature in our world, by default. As eternality in-Christ, becomes the expression of eternality thru Christ within you and me, we become mirrored replications of the *light* and *life* of eternality in our world. The Divine Nature of God is His solution to the Sin problem of mankind. The presence of Divine Nature, in-Christ within us, makes you and me, God's Divine Natured solution to the problem of Sin in our world as well. Be encouraged to engage the *Prospecting Process,* while committing yourself to conducting **R**udiments **of R**esearch exercises often, if not daily. We need your voice to decree and reveal the eternal activity of God in our world, rather than the exercise of communication habits that major on criticism of the church, other religions, or other worldviews. As we major on development of our eternal language, the power of eternality within our language will affect change in our world supernaturally. Our language in-Christ, is already powerful. Our understanding of in-Christ communications, will become even more powerful, efficient, and effective, as we learn how to speak eternally within our ephemeral world. In-Christ, you are an eternal being in an everlasting relationship with our eternal Father and Spirit in heaven, on earth. Since eternality is the foundation for our relationship with the Divine, then let's replicate, represent, manifest, and reveal our foundation, through language that is precise in expression of our eternal foundation. The more we practice speaking eternally, the better we will develop the language of eternality that conduits the eternal intentions of the Throne room on earth, just like Jesus did. Our present Information Age, informs us that everyone has something to say. If this is true, then it is imperative that people, who are <u>OF</u> the eternal, everlasting, Nature of God, in-Christ, speak eternally right now. Eternality in-Christ, has provided you with everything you will need to say. Be encouraged to understand, before being understood. Research, before you speak. Be the character, and expression, of the eternal that you desire to see in our world and know that your labor of love in the study of God's Word through an *Eternal Lens*, will be worth every sacrifice.

A closing prayer is provided, with the hope that it may become a part of your personal constitution, regarding your commitment to becoming a receptacle and vehicle of eternal experience and expression, through the ministry of Christ:

> *Heavenly Father, I am grateful, for every revelation of eternal truth, love, relationship, and activity, that You have provided from heaven, on earth. I am committed to being a vessel and vehicle for Your eternal interest. I exist in-Christ, to participate, partner and companion, Your eternal activity in heaven on earth. I am committed to being Your solution in this world. Thank you, in advance, for opening my eyes daily to see the eternality, that is concealed within the fabric of Your scriptures. I will mirror, the light and revelations of eternality as revealed by Your Spirit, to the world as my daily lifestyle. Thank you for the opportunity to be a change agent, through whom the eternal transforms the ephemeral, in this life. A-men.*

Well, what are you waiting for? Time to begin studying the bible through an *Eternal Lens* with fresh eyes of understanding!

GOD BLESS YOU...

2Ti 2:15 "Be diligent to present thyself approved to God—a workman irreproachable, rightly dividing the word of the truth."

INDEX

- Explain the **Process**, the author referred to on page 11 **in your own words.**

- Explain your understanding of the author's perspective regarding Divine communication with humanity through the Holy Spirit on page 16.

- How are we a *"new species"* in Christ?

SCRIPTURAL ETERNALITY

END OF CHAPTER QUESTIONS FOR CHAPTER TWO

- What does the following declaration mean to you *"What makes us an eternal people of God is the residence of the Divine Nature within us by His Spirit."* (page 18)
- What does the following declaration mean to you, *"the ultimate desires of eternal desires of the Divine are eternal."* (page 19)
- How does living realities, that are everlasting in our present now, advance the transformation of our planet according to Matt 6:10? (page 20,21)
- What is eternal living according to the author on page 21

- How does participation in and with eternal activity result in personal edification? (page 23)

- Explain how alignment with eternal activity occurs with, thru, and AS Oneness with God. (page 23,24)

- Explain your understanding of the following statement, *"Christ majored on revealing the interest of God in this world, we are to do the same."* (page 25).

- What do you look like as a transparent vehicle of eternality in heaven on earth? (page 28)

- Explain some eternal benefits of partnership with the Divine

- How does awareness help you to experience and express the eternal interest of God?

SCRIPTURAL ETERNALITY

END OF CHAPTER QUESTIONS FOR CHAPTER THREE

- Explain the Prospecting Process in your own words as it relates to eternality in the Scriptures.
- Explain the differences between the Prospecting Process and the Rudiments of Research.
- Explain the tools for Rudiment of Research exercises.
- How does Exegesis differ from the Hermeneutic process.
- Explain Participation, Partnership and Companionship from the author's perspective page 57.
- Why do you agree or disagree with the Rudiments of Research *Summary* on page 78.

SCRIPTURAL ETERNALITY

END OF CHAPTER QUESTIONS FOR CHAPTER FOUR

- USE PAGES 80-85 AS A MODEL FOR DISCOVERING ETERNAL PRESENCE OR ACTIVITY IN JOHN 6.

SCRIPTURAL ETERNALITY

END OF CHAPTER QUESTIONS FOR CHAPTER FIVE

- Please explain your understanding of the author's following statement on page 128:

  "Awareness of eternal life, in-Christ, is the experience of my future in my present now, therefore, Christ is the major focus of my life, daily."

- Please explain your understanding of the author's following statement on page 129:

  "Now I understand that Jesus Christ is eternal, and in-Christ, so am I."

- Please explain your understanding of the author's following statement on page 129:

"I will choose to see myself, and the people who possess the Divine Nature of God, as His solution to the Sin problem of humanity in our world."

- Please explain your understanding of the similarities and differences between the author's use of Participation, Partnership, and Companionship (page 130).

- In reference to John 5:17, provide examples of what *joined-in with the work of the Father in heaven, on earth* (page 132), looks like to you.

Congratulations, on the completion of your END OF CHAPTER QUESTIONS.

Please be encouraged to share insights, questions or revelations, relative to your Scriptural Eternality experiences at our website address below:

www.eternallivingnow.com

eternallivingnow77@gmail.com

May the Lord continue to bless you eternally in your present NOW!